CONSOLIDATED B-24 LIBERATOR

Consolidated PB4Y-2 Privateer

Classic WWII Aviation

CONSOLIDATED
B-24 LIBERATOR

General Editor
Edward Shacklady

CERBERUS

Published in 2002

PUBLISHED IN THE UNITED KINGDOM BY:

Cerberus Publishing Limited
Penn House, Leigh Woods
Bristol BS8 3PF
Telephone: ++44 117 974 7175
Facsimile: ++44 117 973 0890
e-mail: cerberusbooks@aol.com

British Library Cataloguing in Publication Data.
A catalogue record for this book is available from the British Library.

ISBN 1 84145 106 1

PRINTED AND BOUND IN ITALY

Contents

Series Introduction   6

Introduction   8

CHAPTER ONE   Development of the Four Engine Bomber   11

CHAPTER TWO   The Liberator is Born   19

CHAPTER THREE   Production Goes into Overtime   29

CHAPTER FOUR   The Liberator in service   47

CHAPTER FIVE   The Oil Targets   71

CHAPTER SIX   The Battle of the Atlantic   77

CHAPTER SEVEN   Other Theatres of Operation   91

CHAPTER EIGHT   The choice of battlefield   107

CHAPTER NINE   The B-24's Escort Fighters   115

CHAPTER TEN   The Liberator Super Bomber   121
                   – the B-32 Dominator

CHAPTER ELEVEN   Camouflage and Markings   135

Appendix A   B-24 Production Plants   139

Appendix B   B-24 Liberator Variants   142

Appendix C   USAAC/USAAF Organizations   146

Appendix D   USAAC/USAAF Groups   148

Appendix E   USAAF B-24 Squadrons   151

Appendix F   RAF B-24 Squadrons   155

Series Introduction

Many different types of aircraft were involved in the Second World War, new, old, conventional, and some, downright bizarre. Any selection in a series of 'classic' aircraft will. therefore, always be arbitrary and subject to the views of individuals. The selection of aircraft for this series has been primarily governed by their operational importance, although some types have, by necessity, other claims for inclusion. The series also seeks to cover a wide spectrum of the different operations involved during the conflict as well as those countries that had a leading role.

The major powers, during the 1930s, were becoming increasingly aware that the political instability throughout the world would inevitably lead to military conflict. The advent of Adolf Hitler's rise to power in Germany, and the increasing strength of the new Luftwaffe, led many nations to the realization that to rely on their air forces' existing capabilities would be extremely unwise and that they had to expand and re-equip with more modern combat aircraft. However, despite this obvious threat no country, at the outbrak of the Second World War, had the numerical strength or modern equipment to compare with that of the Luftwaffe.

The Spanish Civil War (1936-1939) afforded several of the major air powers, particularly Germany and Italy, an ideal opportunity to put their newly designed aircraft to the test under battle conditions. The pilots of Germany's *Legion Condor* and Italy's *Aviazione Legionaria* evolved a number of strategies that were utilized in the early part of the Second World War and the senior officers of the Luftwaffe were quick to realize the need for specialized ground-attack aircraft. On the other hand, the often inferior opposition and the ease with which they were eliminated, gave the German and Italian aircrews, as well as the officials of their respective air forces, an over-estimated view of the superiority of their aircraft.

The Messerschmitt Bf109 had been conceived in the flush of Hitler's take-over of power in 1933, and as a monoplane had complete superiority in the air until the appearance of the Spitfire. Yet the Bf109E, the 'Emil', which provided the main fighter force for Germany during the first year of the Second World War, including the Battle of Britain period, had not evolved significantly from the Bf109C which was the predominant fighter aircraft used by the Luftwaffe in the Spanish Civil War. Italy's pilots had a totally different concept and still preferred the open cockpit and light armoury that would allow them to out-manoeuvre their opponants.

During the immediate pre-war years the peacetime expansion of the Royal Air Force, by comparison with Germany, was slow and hampered by financial restraints. Like Italy, Britain was reluctant to dispense with their bi-plane fighters until the monoplane had proved itself. Although the manufacturers of Britain's two monoplane developments, the Hurricane and the Spitfire, were given substantial pre-war orders the RAF, at the outbreak of war, had little more than 300 Hurricanes in first-line service and approximately 150 Spitfires – less than a tenth of those ordered. In 1938, and with the war clouds gathering, the RAF's weakness was only too apparent and a delegation, the British Purchasing Mission, went to the United States to order substantial quantities of US combat aircraft in an attempt to fill the gap. Most of these aircraft were not delivered until sometime in 1940 and the RAF had to supplement their inferior numbers of Hurricanes and Spitfires with the bi-plane Gloster Gladiator and the near obsolescent Fairey Battle, which were no match for the 'Emil'.

The Soviet Union, although on paper, were numerically strong, its front-line aircraft were anything but modern as it was still in the early stages of a modernization program. Like Britain and France the Soviet Union was relying on aircraft from the United States.

The Japanese, like the Italians, seemed to have a prediliction for open cockpits and lightly armed, but highly manoeuvrable, aircraft. However, they discarded the bi-plane somewhat earlier and, at the time they opened hostilities against the United States, all principle first-line Army and Navy fighters were monoplanes, including the Mitsubishi Zero-Sen.

At the time of Pearl Harbor, in December 1941, the United States' aviation industry was already heavily involved in the production of aircraft for Britain and other countries. This was now substantially increased by the demands of their own forces. Nevertheless output, from 1941 to 1945, included over 12,000 Mustangs, 12,000 Corsairs, 15,000 Thunderbolts and 20,000 Hellcats and Wildcats. In addition over 12,500 B-17s were produced together with over 18,000 B-24 Liberators.

TheClassic WWII Aviation series is designed to give a comprehensive history of many of the aircraft used during this period and each title will cover the prototype development, production and operational use of the aircraft in service with the main protagonists. The series will cover fighter aircraft, heavy, medium and light bombers, in narrative text, many black and white photographs with line and colour drawings to show the different types of aircraft, squadron and unit colour schemes.

Introduction

Following the cessation of hostilities in 1918 the policy of the United States Government between the wars was to be determined by events. These included the failure of the Peace Conference and the harsh application of the Versailles Treaty upon Germany, in particular by the French whose President, Clemenceau, was never to budge an inch from the original, negotiated terms.

As a direct result of this Treaty and its applications Germany collapsed into financial and political chaos with its currency being devalued in a deliberate manoeuvre by various German governments. The political situation deepened with the various Socialist and Communist parties fighting each other and the government forces taking over control of the streets and, eventually, the country.

The precipitous activity that eschewed much of Europe at that time alarmed many of the government and military leaders in the United States and 'isolation' soon became the official American policy. In 1919 this attitude towards Europe and the fact that American forces were involved in several small wars in the Americas created the mood that the American services should be armed for defence purposes only. The United States was determined that never again would their country become involved in a European war, instead a strong deterrent would be created to protect the American homeland.

As part of this policy the US Army Air Service issued a Specification in the early 'twenties called the NBL (or Night Bombardment Long Distance) which attracted two entries. One was the XBNL (Experimental Night Bombardment, Long Distance) Witteman Lewis as designed by Walter Baring. This huge triplane was powered by six x 420-hp Liberty 12A engines, mounted between the mid-upper and lower wings with the four inner engines mounted within two nacelles in tandem and the two outer engines as single tractors. Propellers were two, four-blade pushers (rear inner) and four, two-bladed tractors (outer and inner). However, the aircraft was rejected as its performance was below specification and interest in the long-range bomber soon waned. As a result there was no bombardment aircraft that could be considered as standard for the Army Air Service.

On July 2, 1926, the US Congress passed the Air Corps Act creating the US Army Air Corps (USAAC). Also, a five year modernisation programme was launched with new air units activated, new aircraft purchased and personnel doubled in numbers to 16,500 officers and men.

The organisation of the Air Corps was changed with the Air Service retaining logistical and training responsibility only. The tactical training of combat units and air operations remained the responsibility of ground force commanders to whom the various units were assigned.

In January 1931 the MacArthur-Pratt Agreement was ratified and General MacArthur, as Chief of Staff, allocated responsibility to the Air Corps for the land-based defence of the coast of America. This agreement did not decrease the constant friction that existed between the US Army and Navy, both of whom regarded the defence of the American coastline and territorial possessions as its prerogative. Senior army personnel were convinced that the bomber could be just as effective in this defensive rôle as the navy's ships.

It was an uphill battle, particularly as in 1932 a World Disarmament Conference had taken place in Geneva and the abolition of the bomber as a weapon of war was proposed by the US Delegation – surprisingly this proposal was supported by the majority of nations present. However, Adolf Hitler and his National Socialist Party were well entrenched by January 1933 and political development in Germany and Italy, starting with Germany's withdrawal from Geneva, had prompted a huge arms race in Europe.

The aggressive posturing of Germany, Italy and Japan was taken seriously by the majority of nations and the American Government concluded that a strong air force was necessary to protect its world-wide interests. At that time the American aircraft industry was starved of funds, but both Boeing and Martin had strong industrial bases and the two companies had opened negotiations with the Chief of Staff concerning design studies for a long-range bomber.

One year later, May 1934, the General Staff had approved as its tactical mission 'The Destruction of Distant Land or Naval Targets'. A contract was placed on April 14 with Boeing to design and develop a large, long-range bomber to the Experimental Bomber, Long Range (i.e., the old XBLNR Specification). Wind tunnel tests and mock-up construction were sanctioned that eventually led to an order being placed on January 28, 1935, for the final design and development of the aeroplane. Construction of a prototype started twelve months later.

In the following July the US Government rejected that notion of a separate air force but did agree to the establishment of a General

Headquarters (GHQ) Air Force. This gave control of bombers directly under the command of the US Army Chief. GHQ Air Force was equal in status to that of the Chief of the Air Corps, who continued to administer supply while training procedures were the responsibility of the Chief of Staff.

The urgent need for fighting aircraft for the turbulent nations of the European Continent was highlighted when Germany, rejecting the Versailles Treaty, started the rapid process of rearmament. The embryonic *Luftwaffe* was made possible due to the training facilities available with the aid of the Russian Government, and the knowledge acquired during the production of quasi-civil airliners, such as the Dorniers and Junkers, which could be quickly transformed into bombers.

Combined with the experience gained by *Luftwaffe* personnel when fighting in the Condor Legion during the Spanish Civil War of the late 1930s, the German war machine at that time led the world in military aviation.

Fortunately all was not lost as Britain, ever watchful of developments in Europe, was able to catch up quickly once public money was liberally made available to spend on new designs and expansion of large factories under the Shadow Factory Schemes. The motorcar industry, in particular, quickly switched from producing for the civil market to the military. The engine companies expanded at a similar rate.

However, it was not until the production strength of America was established after the Japanese attack on Pearl Harbor that the supply of sufficient aeroplanes for the Allies was undertaken. This provocative move by Japan forced America into a war it did not want to fight but, having been forced to defend interests in the Pacific, its industry quickly made up the deficit suffered by the armed forces during the Depression years of the 'twenties and early 'thirties.

When America joined the war in December 1941 its heavy-bomber force rested upon one, four-engined bomber, namely the Boeing B-17 'Fortress', which had entered service just months before war started in Europe in 1939. The Liberator was to follow. In order to understand just how these two bombers were ready for action within months of the Japanese attack we should take a look at their backgrounds.

CHAPTER ONE

Development of the Four Engine Bomber

In May 1934 the Army Air Corps issued a directive for a requirement of a bomber with a range of 5,000 miles, a bomb load of 2,000 lbs., at a speed of between 200 and 250 mph. The authorities had decided on these parameters after assessing that immediate, and longer term needs were to have aircraft that could defend US interests in Panama as well as provide a defensive force for their further flung territories such as Alaska and Hawaii. The directive became known as 'Project A' and the Boeing Aeroplane Company received a development contract that resulted in a design, Model 294, a large, four-engined, aircraft. In June 1936 the Army Air Corps, after approving the designs and preliminary work, ordered one prototype under the designation XBLR-1. This designation was subsequently changed to XB-15, and the prototype, serial 35-277, made its first flight on October 15, 1937.

Many new innovations were incorporated into the design such as heated crew quarters, rest bunks, kitchen and toilet. The power generators, for these operations, were driven by two, small petrol engines. A crew of five flew this monster of 35 tons.

The design was originally drawn up to install four Allison V-03420 in-line, liquid-cooled engines and scale, mock-up examples, were installed in the full sized mock-up of the prototype. In the event, the Allisons were never used and were replaced by four, 1,000-hp Pratt & Whitney R-1830s air-cooled radials.

With these engines the huge prototype could only reach a maximum speed of 197mph, due mainly to the drag of the thick wing section. However, the plus side was that it could fly at 28,850 feet and carry a load of 2,511 lbs. over a range of 5,130 miles. This, though, was at a time when the Spitfire and the Messerschmitt Bf 109 prototypes were reaching speeds of almost 300mph. Notwithstanding this, the US General Staff considered that the Boeing bomber met their conditions of carrying a one ton load over 5,000 miles.

Two service models, known as the Y1B-20, were ordered and had the increased power Pratt & Whitney R-2180 air-cooled engines. However, these pre-production prototypes were cancelled. The sole prototype was delivered to the Air Corps during 1937 after maker's trials and it was finally converted into a cargo carrier with the new designation of XC-105.

Leading particulars XB-15

Wing span: 149ft. 0in., area; 2,780sq.ft. Length: 87ft. Height: 18ft. 11in. Weights: tare; 37,700lbs., gross; 70,700lbs. Max speed: 197mph. @ 5,000ft, cruise; 152mph. Ceiling: 20,990ft. Range: 3,400 miles. Engine: 4 x Pratt & Whitney Twin Wasp R-1830-11s. Fuel: 4,190 gallons. Armament: two x 0.50in. and four x .303in. guns in nose, dorsal turret, two waist blisters, ventral forward and rear guns in fuselage. Bomb load: 12,000lbs. It had been intended to replace the Pratt & Whitney R-1830s with increased hp engines.

The Martin Company had also submitted a design to the same specification for a fast, long-range, heavy bomber to be powered by four Allison in-line V-1710 engines submerged into a thick wing section, each engine driving a three bladed propeller of 12ft 3in diameter by extension shafts. Known as the Martin Model 145a, XB-16, it had a broad chord centre section accommodating the engines, with the wing leading edge swept back on the outer panels. The wing was mounted low on to the smooth, streamlined fuselage while the tail unit was a broad chord unit with twin fins and rudders.

This proposal was rejected as the Air Corps had the XB-17 prototype that was preferred, but Martin quickly reacted by submitting a second design, which was in total contrast to its predecessor. It, too, made use of a broad chord, equi-tapered wing configuration but had two booms supporting the twin fin/rudder tailplane. The main fuselage was situated under the wing and it contained the crew quarters, controls and large bomb bay.

Prototype YB-17

Leading particulars XB-16

Wing span: 140ft. 0in., area: 2,600sq.ft. Length: 84ft. 0in. Height: 19ft. 7in. Weights: tare; 31,957lbs., gross; 65,000lbs., useful load; 33,045lbs. Max speed: 237mph. @ 22,500ft., cruise; 120mph. Ceiling: 22,500ft. Range: 6,200 miles. Endurance: 42 hours. Engines: four x 1,150-hp Allison V-1710s. Fuel: 4,238 gallons. Crew of ten. Armament: in glazed nose position plus four retractable dorsal and ventral turrets. Bomb load: 12,190lbs.

It was to be powered by six Allison V-1710-3 engines each of 1,150-hp with four buried in the wing leading edges driving propellers by means of extension shafts. The two outer nacelles continued over the wing to the trailing edges where the two additional engines were installed as pushers. They, too, were driven via extension shafts. At 52 tons it was the heaviest of the three designs.

The Giant Douglas XB-19

The history of GHQ Air Force in relation to the four-engined, long-range, heavy bomber is closely related to the changing concept of air power and the gradual acceptance by the die-hard Army Generals of the strategic potential of long-range bombardment.

During 1935 both the Army and Navy regarded the heavy bomber as a defensive weapon with little long-term strategy. But one individual, General Andrews, with considerable foresight, suggested that all future bombers be of the four-engined type and this was to finally lead to the first capable four-engine bomber, the Boeing B-17. However, before continuing with its place in history it is necessary to fit into the overall picture the effect of the Douglas XBLR-2, the second true bomber to the old specification.

Design of the Douglas bomber started when a contract was placed with the giant Douglas Company for the design of yet another four-engined bomber in the mould of the Boeing XB-15. Design was initiated on October 31, 1935, and a prototype ordered. A wooden mock-up, with four, dummy Allison engines, was to reach completion in March 1936.

By then, costs were beginning to spiral out of control and Douglas requested an opt-out from the Army contract. The Air Corps, however, insisted that the company proceed with the design and eventually the prototype aeroplane was delivered with Douglas having spent $4 million on the project. Such was the size and complexity of the basic airframe that the prototype did not fly until June 1937, by which time the Fortress was in service and design of the B-29 initiated.

The prototype XB-19 was delivered to the Air Corps in November 1941 but performance, even when powered by four x 2,000-hp Wright R-3350-5 18-cylinder Cyclone engine was poor. Defensive armament was impressive with no less than twelve machine-guns, located in nose and top forward turrets, equipped with one x 37mm cannon and one x .303in machine-gun, single 0.50in machine-guns on each side of the bombardier's position and in the fuselage sides. The total amount of ammunition was to be limited to 4,700 rounds.

The XBLR Class Super Bomber, as it was now being termed, was not meeting the requirements and the Second Series had ended with the Douglas XB-19/19A designs. Another large aircraft company, Sikorsky, was interested in submitting a design as it was skilled in the design of very large aeroplanes such as their long range 'Clipper Class' flying boats, many of them serving with Pan American Airlines.

Leading particulars XB-19

Wing span: 212ft. 1in., area; 4,285sq.ft. Length: 132ft. 4in. Height: 42ft. 0in. Weights: tare; 84,431lbs., gross; 160,332lbs. Max speed: 204mph., cruise; 135mph. (185 with Allison engines). Ceiling: 39,900ft. Range: 7,710 miles. Engines: four x 2,000-hp Wright R-3350-5, 18-cylinder Cyclones. Fuel: 10,400 gallons. Armament: as above. Bomb load: 16,000lbs. internal, plus bombs on external racks.

The company was considered a strong contender to provide an XBLR and

Prototype YB-17

when their submission was examined it was found to be an elegant design which met with the approval of the Air Corps. On February 29, after the Air Corps had placed a contract for a prototype, work started on the design, development and construction of a wooden mock-up. It was examined by Air Corps Officers the following March but they were not impressed, even considering that the Douglas XB-19 was the better proposition.

Leading particulars XBLR-3

Wing span: 205ft. 0in., area; 4,624sq.ft., aspect ratio; 8:11, a wide span, narrow chord design. Length: 120ft. 0in. Height: 35ft. 0in. Gross weight: 119,770lbs. Max speed: 229mph., cruise; 199mph. Ceiling: 18,200ft. Range: 7,650 miles. Duration: six hours. Engines: four x 1,600-hp Allison XV-4320-1s. Propeller: three speed CS. Fuel: 3,900 gallons. No armament details.

In August 1934, while Boeing were still in the design stages for the XB-15 the Army Air Corps had, apparently, 're-thought' the situation and a new directive, USAAC Circular 35-26, was issued to the aircraft industry. The directive announced a competition requesting designs with detailed specifications for a multi-engined, coastal defence aircraft capable of carrying a 2,000 lbs. bomb-load, but this time over a reduced range of at least 1,000 miles and at a speed between 200 and 250mph. The Air Corps had lowered its sights on getting an XBLR, but the decision was to lead to the provision of two, four engined bombers for the Air Corps, the Fortress and, eventually, the Liberator.

It was also specified that all entrants to the competition had to be built and flown to Wright Field for evaluation by August 1935. To meet this extreme deadline many manufacturers decided to concentrate on twin-engine aircraft – a number of which were already in hand. But the Boeing Aeroplane Company, of Seattle, Washington, was in a unique position to respond successfully to the competition as it was supplying both fighter and bomber aircraft to the Army Air Corps and the Navy. After a study of the specification the company decided that four engines would be the minimum required, despite its experience with the XB-15.

The new Boeing design was smaller that the XB-15 and carried a reduced bomb load but the range was equal to that demanded by the Wright Field requirements. Preliminary designs of what was initially called the 'Model 299' started on June 18, 1934, and construction of a prototype on August 16, with it being rolled out on July 17, 1935. The time factor was short but it must be recalled that building the XB-15 had provided the company with extensive knowledge of how to build a large bomber.

The first flight of Model 299, now known as the XB-17 although no official military designation had yet been given, was made on July 28, 1935. On August 20, it was delivered to Wright Field for evaluation against the Douglas Model DB-1, which was based upon their civil DC-2 transport. There was also a surprise entry, the Martin Model 146, an improved version of their B-10 bomber. This was, however, hardly in the same class as its rivals despite it being in service with the Air Corps.

The Boeing prototype crashed during the flight demonstration as a ground crew member had forgotten to remove an elevator control lock. But the USAAC had been sufficiently impressed by the XB-17's performance and had recommended the Model 299 to the General Staff for series production – its progeny to become the 'Flying Fortress'.

Just over one year later that same General Staff had become concerned over the generous allocation of funds for the Air Corps, in particular the funding for the heavy bomber. Expenditure of funds for ground forces had been cut in order to expand the aircraft production programme. Also, the Generals preferred the Douglas DB-I to the Boeing as they regarded the former as an all-purpose bomber, and it cost forty percent less than the Model 299.

A $6 million budget had been allocated for the Air Corp's heavy bomber programme in fiscal year 1936 but this was cut to $3.5 million for the period 1938 to June 1939. This reduction in funding was implemented despite President Roosevelt allowing the Air Corp's expenditure to rise from $17.4 to $50.9 million because of the European situation. The General Staff were not convinced by the debate and were more concerned with quantity than quality. They placed an order with Douglas for 133 production aircraft as the B-18, while Boeing received a smaller order for 13 test Model 299 Fortresses. The four-engine bomber programme had received a shock.

By default the USAAC had received its first four-engined bomber although it could easily have been a force armed primarily with medium twin-engined types had the Generals had their way. The stakes were raised in early 1938 for as the crisis in Europe heightened the US War Department altered the defence posture. It was decided that military forces should be brought to a state of readiness to attack an enemy homeland and destroy their industrial base in the belief that this would force the civilian population to bring to an end any war. The case for the larger bomber had been strengthened but the scenario that bombing would force any civil population to make its government sue for peace proved to be a fallacy.

Air Force General Spaatz was quoted as stating that Japan, which was pursuing an aggressive policy in China, could only be attacked from the air by large, four-engined bombers carrying an adequate bomb load. The American bomber could, by extending its range, be based in the Philippines, Siberia or the Aleutians. The definition of the eventual enemy was correct, the location of bomber bases wrong. Other than the Boeing Fortress there was no other US bomber available that could fly the distances demanded, and carry a suitable weight of bombs.

In the same year the USAAC was considering a new dimension of aerial bombing, that of the pinpoint-attack in daylight from high altitudes at specific targets such as industrial and military bases. The bombers would protect themselves by means of hundreds of guns in self-protecting formations.

CHAPTER TWO

The Liberator is Born

The European War provided the impetus for a second large, long range, multi-engined bomber although when America entered the war there did not appear to be any requirement for the development of a second.

The US Army Air Corps was looking into the future for an eventual replacement for their B-17, and that replacement was required to have an overall improved performance. A speed of 300mph plus was recommended with the ability to carry a greater load of bombs. In addition, a range and fuel for 3,000 miles, a ceiling of 35,000ft and a heavy defensive armament.

A step along the long road to producing a second contemporary bomber was the work completed by the Consolidated Aircraft Company. Their Model 32 was, initially, unconnected with any bomber project associated with the USAAC and started at the request of the French Government in May 1938. They had issued a specification to Consolidated, who were then based in San Diego, California, after moving from Buffalo, New York, in 1935/36, for a long distance bomber

The resurgence of the German Luftwaffe under command of Hermann Göring, had caused the French Government to become aware of the shortcomings of the bomber arm of the *Armée de l'air*. It did not possess a true heavy bomber and when the need to acquire one became urgent the French aircraft industry was working to capacity on numerous warplane designs, none of which would have been ready for series production for many years.

American aircraft manufacturers were relatively under-employed and could easily apply considerable effort to the task of building, even designing, new fighting aircraft from scratch. More to the point their production methods could outstrip the best in Europe.

Consolidated's first effort for a heavy bomber design to the French

Specification was the Model 32, clearly based upon their new Model 29 flying boat, the PB2Y, then under development for the US Navy, and in every aspect a land based variant.

As the design progressed into 1939 the USAAC also drew up its requirements for the new heavy bomber as part of the VLR (Very Long-Range) bomber scheme. This new design was to be superior in performance to the, then, new B-17 Fortress which was just entering series production. The specification demanded an aeroplane with a minimum speed in excess of 300mph at its best operational height, a range of 3,000 miles and ceiling of 35,000ft. At that time the new design was to introduce a number of novel features such as the tri-cycle undercarriage, the main units of which retracted sideways due to the thin section of the Davis wing.

At around the same period Consolidated had been approached by USAAC with a proposal that they set up a second source production line for the B-17. However, the Chief Designer of Consolidated was convinced that the Model 32 was the better aeroplane in many respects and could be altered to fulfil the VLR scheme. The company seized the opportunity to initiate a design study as an entry for that Specification.

The finished result was a second design similar to the French Specification and using the same high speed Davis, high-aspect-ratio wing and twin fin/rudder rear section of their Model 31 P4Y-1 flying boat. By January 1939 the company presented its preliminary specification of their Model 32 to the Commanding General, U.S.A.A.C., H.H. ('Hap') Arnold, and the company was directed to develop and build the new bomber under the designation XB-24.

Although the overall fuselage design, for the XB-24, was relatively conventional the wing was shoulder-mounted allowing easy loading in the fuselage and maximum bomb stowage. Another innovative feature was the main undercarriage stowed in the mainplanes with blister fairings covering the wheels when retracted. The nose-wheel undercarriage could be retracted into the fuselage at the front of the aircraft and, after consideration, it was decided the tail unit would be a twin fin and rudder assembly similar to Consolidated's flying boat, Model 31.

The wing and tail configuration gave stability for precision bombing, although the control of these assemblies, for maximum effect, put additional strain on the pilot. The central bomb-bay could take up to 8,000 lbs. of bombs that could be vertically stowed in two compartments, fore and aft. The fuselage keel beam ran down the centre of the bomb-bays creating a central aisle or 'walkway' for access. The bomb doors were unique in that they were two roller-type segment halves that opened and upwardly retracted into the fuselage.

The XB-24's fuselage, in contrast to the B-17 and other bombers of that period, offered immense storage capabilities and subsequent production models of the B-24 utilised this in its many adaptations. Unlike the B-17, however, armament was limited to a small number of 0.3in. Browning machine-guns, one mounted in the transparent nose, two more each side of the fuselage where movable hatches allowed access. A fourth was housed in a 'cupola' at the rear end of the fuselage.

Tests of models in the wind tunnel took place in February and the design team visited Wright Field to hold further discussions with senior Air Corps personnel. A contract was signed on March 30, 1939, for the Model 32, XB-24 prototype after the company had incorporated almost 30 design changes to meet Air Corps requirements.

The USAAC now had a second heavy-bomber design and, shortly before the prototype contract had been issued, they placed an order for

Close up view of underside of C-109 Liberator tanker showing roller doors.

seven YB-24s. This type differed from the XB-24 in having an increased gross weight and de-icing boots on the wings and tail, with a maximum speed 275mph. A second order for 38 B-24A production models was also given for evaluation purposes. France also agreed with the design and decided to place an order for 120 Model 32 bombers. This order was to be eventually diverted to England when France surrendered to Germany in May 1940, but the British Government seeing the potential of this bomber had already, in early 1940, ordered 164. When completed the aircraft, initially intended for France, were converted to RAF standards and were known as the LB-30A, which on arrival in England became known as the 'Liberator' – a name that was also adopted later by the US Army Air Corps. Originally the name 'Eagle' had been favoured by Consolidated and then the name 'Conqueror' had been considered but rejected as the US Congress thought it was too aggressive.

Before being shipped to Europe twenty-five finished aircraft were retained by USAAC after the Japanese attack on Pearl Harbor. Fifteen, still bearing RAF serial numbers, were despatched to the Pacific Theatre but none reached the Philippines before the Japanese occupation. The Liberators were ferried through Africa and India and eventually reached the 7th Bombardment Group in Java.

The XB-24 (39-680) fitted with self-sealing fuel tanks and much improved turbo-supercharged R-1830-41 engines.

The prototype bomber for the USAAC had made its first flight on December 29, 1939, as the XB-24 (serial 39-680) powered by four 1200-hp Pratt & Whitney Twin Wasp R-1830-33 engines. The flight tests revealed a maximum speed of 273mph instead of the 311 estimated, even when mechanical superchargers were installed. Although below the speed of the B-17 Fortress the XB-24s potential range was considerable. They were delivered for service trials but only nine were completed to B-24 standards. The urgent need for bombers, by both France and Great

Britain, meant that six YB-24s and 20 B-24As were hurriedly delivered to England.

The first RAF LB-30A (AM258) made its initial flight on January 17, 1941. This was followed by five additional ones (AM259-AM263) that were used, from March 1941 onwards, in an unarmed transport rôle with the newly created Trans-Atlantic Return Ferry Service. With their range and endurance they were the only aircraft capable of flying between Prestwick and Montreal non-stop – a journey of just under 3,000 miles. Four of these aircraft continued as long-range transport with the British Overseas Airways Corporation (BOAC) carrying civil registration (AM258 as G-AGDR, AM259 as G-AGCD, AM262 as G-AGHG and AM263 as G-AGDS).

An additional batch of 20 production LB-30As were delivered to the RAF in mid-1941. These were designated Liberator Is (AM910-AM929), and were the first to be put in to operational service. The RAF Coastal Command extensively modified the aircraft and fitted it with the ASV radar system requiring a number of aerials, four of which, were fixed to the top of the rear fuselage. In addition the standard armament of 0.3in. machine-guns was increased by four 20mm. Hispano cannons fitted under the cockpit section of the nose.

No. 120 Squadron of RAF Coastal Command, based at Nutt's Corner, Belfast, were the first to receive the Liberator I in June 1941. These aircraft were classified as VLR (Very Long-Range) and had an operational range of 2,400 miles.

In the same month, June 1941, the US Army Air Force (recently changed from the Army Air Corps) took delivery of its first B-24A aircraft. Although 38 had been ordered only nine were delivered as the

Liberator GR. Mk III of No. 120 Squadron, RAF Coastal Command.

remainder were needed for conversions.

The B-24As that were received by the USAAF had a similar configuration to the Liberator Is of the RAF except that the armament was increased by having six 0.5in. machine-guns and twin 0.3in. guns in the tail.

The USAAC had no counterpart to the Liberator II, the next mark of aircraft ordered by the RAF from Consolidated. It differed from the Liberator I by having increased armament but also an additional section in the fuselage nose was inserted ahead of the cockpit – this added approximately 2ft 6in. to the overall length of the aircraft. The two hand-held gun positions, each side of the fuselage, were replaced by Boulton Paul power-operated turrets that held four 0.303in. Browning machine-guns each. One turret was installed in the mid-upper position while the other in the rear fuselage. Curtiss Electric propellers with blade pitch-change motors replaced the Hamilton Hydromatic propellers found in the Liberator I but the maximum speed was reduced to 263mph caused by the additional drag of the gun turrets.

Liberator GR. Mk VI of No. 220 Squadron, RAF Coastal Command.

In total 139 Liberator IIs (AL503-AL641) were delivered to Nos 120, 59 and 86 Squadron of RAF Coastal Command in addition to three operational with No. 159 Squadron, RAF Bomber Command, (AL526, AL564, AL600), and four with No. 160 Squadron, (AL555, AL563, AL582, AL630), in the Middle East. These two squadrons became the first bomber units to operate this type of aircraft and, indeed, the Liberator II can be considered the first operational bomber type of this illustrious family of aircraft. Included in these totals were the unarmed variants, designated LB-30s, that were used for transport by the Trans-Atlantic Return Ferry Service and BOAC while another, AL504, became the personal transport of the British Prime Minister, Winston Churchill, and was given the name 'Commando'.

Winston Churchill had this Mk II Liberator 'Commando', for his personal transport. This was one of the few Liberators with a single tail fin/rudder.

Leading particulars LB-30

Wing span: 110ft., area; 1048sq.ft. Length: 66ft. 4in. Height: 18ft. 0in. Weights: tare; 37,000lbs, gross; 62,000lbs. Max speed: 263mph. @ 20,000ft. Ceiling: 24,000ft. Time-to-height: 20,000ft. in 40mins. Range: 990 miles. Bomb load: 12,880lbs. Engines: four x Pratt & Whitney R-1830-S3C-4 of 1,000-hp @ 12,500ft. Crew of eight. Armament:. Two x 0.50in. machine-guns in nose, dorsal and tail turrets, plus one 0.50in. at ventral and waist positions. NTU contract 12464 of April 26, 1939 diverted to RAF under BR-5068, December 16, 1940. RAF serial, AM258-263, six aircraft. LB-30B Contract BR-F-677 of June 4, 1940 as Liberator. RAF serials ASM910-929, 20 aircraft. San Diego.

Leading particulars LB-24

Wing span: 103ft. 9in, area; 1420sq.ft. Length: 68ft. 4in. Height: 18ft. 4in. Weights: tare; 26,520lbs. gross; 37,000lbs. max.; 45,650lbs. Max speed: 295mph. @ 25,000ft., cruise; 230mph., landing; 78mph. Ceiling: 38,000ft. Time-to-height: 10,000ft. in 7.8 mins. Range; 2,400 miles with 4,000 lbs. bombs, max.; 3,600 miles. Engines: four x Wright R-1829-51 of 1,000-hp @ T/O, 800-hp @ 25,000ft. Fuel: 1,700 to 2,492 gallons. One built under Contract 12456 of 30 March 1939, serial 39-556. San Diego.

Leading particulars B-24A

Wing span: 110ft. 0in., area; 1048sq.ft. Length: 18ft. 6in. Weights: tare; 30,000lbs. gross; 39,345lbs. max: 53,600lbs. Max speed: 292.5 mph. @ 15,000ft., cruise; 228mph., landing; 92mph. Ceiling: 32,000ft. Initial rate of climb: 1,780ft/min. Time-to-height: 10,000ft. in 5.6 mins. Range: 2,200 miles. Max. 4,000 miles @ 190mph. Engines: four x 1,200-hp. Pratt & Whitney R-1830-33 (S3C4-G), mechanically supercharged. Fuel: 2,150 to 3,100 gallons. Crew of 8/10. Armament: six x 0.50in and two x .30in. machine-guns. Bombs 4,000lbs. Contract 13281 of 10 August 1939 for 38 aircraft. Twenty-three aircraft as B-24C/D. Serials 40-2369 to 2377. San Diego.

B-24D Formating Monitor, 2nd Bombardment Division, 8th Air Force.

Close-up view of nose art.

B-24M, 459th Bombardment Group, 15th Air Force, with 'Shark Mouth' motif on nose.

B-24M, 461st Bombardment Group, 756th Squadron, 15th Air Force, Italy.

B-24M Chinese Nationalist Air Force.

B-24M, 451996, with odd fuselage number of BC-922.

CHAPTER THREE

Production Goes into Overtime

The flight trials, in 1940, of the XB-24B resulted from the development of the original XB-24 prototype. For these trials the original mechanically supercharged Pratt & Whitney R-183033 engines were replaced by four of their 1200-hp turbo-supercharged R-1830-41 (S4C4-G) engines. The turbo-superchargers were positioned on the lower surface of the engine nacelles and the oil coolers relocated to the sides of the front cowlings. This new configuration gave an overall elliptical appearance to the cowlings that became a characteristic feature of the Liberator. The new engines now gave an increased speed of 310mph (273mph for the XB-30).

After the successful trials a small batch of nine B-24Cs was produced. These were equipped with the Hamilton Hydromatic propellers and, additionally, a Martin dorsal gun-turret and a Consolidated tail-turret, with each turret having two 0.5in. machine-guns installed.

From this small number of aircraft evolved the first large-scale production variant, the B-24D, which also became the first of an illustrious family to enter operational service with the bombing units of the US Army Air Force.

The B-24D, apart from some minor changes and the installation of the 1200-hp Pratt & Whitney 1830-43 engines, was put into production among the various factories opened by Consolidated. The US government's required target of 2000 heavy bombers per month required the immediate setting-up of many more production plants. Therefore, with government assistance, Consolidated, in addition to their San Diego, California, (CO) plant where 2425 B-24D s were built, set up production with a plant at Fort Worth, Texas, (CF) which built 303 B-24Ds. The Douglas Aircraft Company at Tulsa, Oklahoma, (DT), also built ten of this variant with the Ford Motor Company also being requested to take some

B-24D, 272869, of the 93rd Bombardment Group, with early type of fuselage national markings.

of the production of the aircraft's components at their new, large, plant at Willow Run. As the programme was expanded Ford were committed to produce a minimum of 200 completed B-24Ds per month, and an additional 150 in parts to be assembled elsewhere.

These production B-24Ds remained consistent in their original configuration, albeit various batches had different armament variations, but the final batches of some 37 aircraft were fitted with the 100-hp Pratt

B-24D 'Hellsadroppin'. of the 93rd Bombardment Group, 8th Air Force (ETO).

& Whitney R-1839-65 engine.

The normal take-off weight of the late series B-24Ds was 64,000 lbs. with a 5,000 lbs. bomb load and a maximum speed of 303 mph at 25,000ft. The range at this speed was 1,800 miles within a lapsed time of $7^1/_2$ hours.

In mid-1942 the RAF received 260 B-24Ds, with slight modifications, which were designated Liberator III and IIIAs (249 BZ711-BZ959 and 11 LV336-LV346).

Most of these aircraft went on the strength of RAF Coastal Command and proved to be extremely successful in combating the growing U-boat menace. Some of the later batches of B-24s were extensively modified and supplied to Coastal Command as Liberator GR.Vs (32 FK214-FK245 and 90 FL906-FL995). These aircraft were fitted with radar equipment, including chin and retractable ventral radomes, and, in addition to the ASV equipment and aerials, they now had the Leigh Light, installed under the starboard wing, for night time detection of surfaced submarines. A small number had eight rockets mounted, in groups of four, on brackets attached to the forward fuselage.

The B-24D was also used for anti-submarine duties by the US Army Air Force from bases on the US Atlantic seaboard. Several of these units were subsequently moved to Newfoundland, North Africa and Britain, where they successfully continued their anti-submarine duties.

In August 1943 the US Navy was given governmental approval to take over all anti-submarine Liberators, having already had some of these

B-24D (128702) of the 98th Bombardment Group.

aircraft diverted from the USAAF in 1942. These aircraft were used for maritime reconnaissance and designated PB4Y-1s. When the USAAF's Anti-Submarine Command was disbanded on August 31, 1943, they exchanged all their ASV equipped Liberators for an equal amount of non-modified Liberators from the US Navy. Soon after the two USAAF anti-submarine squadrons, attached to the RAF Coastal Command in Britain,

B-24D, 376th Bombardment Group, 15th Air Force, flies past Vesuvius, Italy.

were replaced by three squadrons of the US Navy now flying the re-designated PB4Y-1.

The Liberator, with its extensive range, became the mainstay in the Pacific Theatre of Operations. From its arrival in January 1942, to help evacuate British troops with their withdrawal from Java, until mid-1944 when it was, more-or-less, supplemented by the B-29 Superfortress, the Liberator was supreme. Later in 1942 the first B-24Ds were delivered to that area and, with their turbo-superchargers and increased armament, became more than a match against the Japanese fighters. By 1943 the Liberator had almost replaced the Fortress in the area as the standard USAAF long-range heavy bomber.

The USAAF, following the success of the early Liberator's rôle as a modified transport aircraft, ordered a number to be converted for specialised logistics duties. Replacing the bomb-bay area Consolidated installed a passenger compartment that could, with little difficulty, be further changed to accommodate freight. The nose and tail guns were removed, and a door on the port side, approximately six feet square, allowed access for loading. Adapted from the B-24D the production of the C-87 'Liberator Express' first commenced at the Fort Worth plant in April 1942, ultimately to be transferred to San Diego in 1944. 276 of these aircraft were produced for the USAAF and, with a crew of five, could accommodate 20 passengers. The RAF received 24 of these (EW611-EW634) but insisted that they incorporated a line of windows each side of the fuselage. These operated with RAF Transport Command as the Liberator C.VII. They performed a similar rôle for the US Navy as RY-2s and five operated as AT-22s (later designated TB-24s) for flight engineer training duties. In addition the USAAF ordered a further six aircraft, designated C-87A, to carry 16 VIP passengers with sleeping accommodation.

B-24D 'Chug A Lug' of the 98th Bombardment Group.

A proposed armed transport, C-87B, was never produced but another use, under the designation C-109, was as a flying tanker providing fuel for the B-29 Superfortresses that later operated out of China.

B-24D, 7th Bombardment Group, 10th Air Force.

When, in 1942, the Ford Motor Company's plant at Willow Run opened it started by producing B-24Es, a late model 'D' with modified propellers. In all 791 B-24Es were produced – 480 by the Willow Run plant. Although there is no evidence that the RAF received any of this variant they had reserved the designation 'Liberator IV' for them.

A variant, XB-24F, was to be a late model 'D' with a thermal de-icing system but this never reached production.

Later in 1942 the Dallas plant of North American Aviation was opened and, again working from the late model B-24D specifications, produced another variant, the B-24G. The first batch of five were the first Liberators to replace the hand-held guns in the nose with a power-operated turret

B-24D, 41-23659 'Blonde Bomber II', piloted by Lt Don Story, made a forced landing on February 20, 1943 and was captured. Note the British fin flash.

that housed twin 0.5in. machine-guns. Subsequent production batches also incorporated the R-1830-65 engine and the bomb-load facility was raised to 12,800 lbs. In all 430 B-24Gs were built at Dallas.

Consolidated's Fort Worth plant built 738 of the next variant, the B-24H, with the first batch (B-24H-1 CF to B-24H-15 CF) having the Emerson electrically-operated nose-turret fitted. 1,780 of this type were built by Ford's Willow Run plant and 582 by Douglas but all were fitted with the hydraulic powered Consolidated nose-turret.

The RAF, under the designation 'Liberator VI', received 40 B-24H aircraft (BZ960-BZ999) and were operating with both Coastal Command and Bomber Command. Twelve squadrons in the Middle East operated this variant, while 14 squadrons in the Far East were similarly equipped. For the Liberator VI the Consolidated tail-turret was replaced by a standard Boulton Paul turret, that accommodated four 0.303in. machine-guns, but retained the Emerson nose-turret.

Of all the variants the B-24J was built in the largest quantities. 6,678

B-24II during routine training.

were constructed utilising the five plants that had previously been engaged on the production of the B-24.

There was little difference between the 'J' and the previous variant – the A-5 autopilot was replaced by the C-1 and the S-1 gun-sight replaced by the M-9, but all were fitted with the R-1830-65 Pratt & Whitney engine. Some later batch aircraft were fitted with a GE B-22 turbo-supercharger

B-24H, 392nd Bombardment Group.

that enhanced altitude performance.

The USAAF, by September 1944, had 6,043 B-24s in operational service and equipped 45 of their bomber groups overseas. Although somewhat deficient in armament, where this weakness was shown in the northern European Theatre, it performed well in the Mediterranean and Pacific operations.

The B-24J was also taken up by the RAF, who received 1,200 under the designations 'Liberator B' and 'GR.VII', and a number of these had their gun-turrets removed to converted for freight-carrying duties. Known as Liberator C.VI and C.VII some were also employed in the 'Carpetbagger' special duties missions where they were used to drop agents and supplies behind enemy lines. Included in this number, many went to Commonwealth air forces such as Australia, Canada and South Africa.

Production of the B-24 went on unabated with the introduction of the

B-24J 'Screamin Meemie', 451st Bombardment Group, Ploesti, 15 July 1944.

B-24L. Again this variant differed very little from the previous model, 'J', other than having a repositioned tail-turret with manually-operated 0.5in. machine-guns that gave a wider field of fire. During 1944 Consolidated built 417 at their San Diego plant, and Ford 1,250 at Willow Run.

The USAAF's orders for the B-24M proved to be the last large-scale production version of the Liberator. By this time renumbered variants had only small modifications, primarily in armament. The B-24M, being

Note the modified nose section on this B-24L. In Sea Search camouflage.

no exception, the manually-operated tail guns were replaced by Motor Products' lightweight, power-operated, twin-gun-turret. 916 B-24Ms were built by Consolidated-Vultee Company, including the 6,725th and last to be produced at San Diego, and 1,677 by Ford at Willow Run.

During the Liberator's evolution a number of variations were designed and were left at this stage of development. The B-24N nearly became one of these but went into production in April 1944. For some time the USAAF had been arguing that the Liberator with a single tail

B-24M, 461st Bombardment Group, with Red tail markings. Note feathered propeller.

would provide greater stability, although all previous variants with he twin-tail had achieved great approbation throughout their working life in many theatres of operation. In 1943, Ford modified a B-24D (42-40234) by replacing the familiar tail with a large, single, square-cut vertical configuration. It also incorporated a more powerful 1350-hp Pratt & Whitney R-1830-75 engine. With a few modifications to its armament the XB-24K, as it was designated, could fly 11mph faster with a greatly improved climb rate than previous variants.

Therefore, in April 1944, it was decided that all future Liberators would have this single vertical tail and a slightly redesigned XB-24K became the XB-24N. These modifications amounted to repositioning the nose and tail guns. In addition to the prototype XB-24N (44-48753) there were seven YB-24Ns built at Willow Run by Ford before production

PBY-1. Yellow overall. Converted by US Navy modification unit.

ceased altogether on May 31, 1945 as the war ended.

Outstanding orders for 5,168 B-24Ns were cancelled, although some 740 aircraft of a US Navy development for the single tail Liberator were delivered. This was the PB4Y-2 Privateer, the original contract having been placed in May 1943.

The first of the PB4Y-1s were delivered in June 1944 after an order for 600 had been placed in October 1943. The first examples were delivered to the US Navy's squadrons VPB-118 and 119, and overseas deployment started on 6 January 1945 when VPB-118 left for operations in Tinbian, in the Mariannas. By the end of the war thirteen squadrons were eventually equipped and five operated a combination of PB4Y-2 and the navalised Liberator.

At least nineteen aircraft were converted to PB4Y-2B standards which could carry two 1,600 lbs. ASM-N-2 Bat radar guided bombs, one stored under each main wing, for strikes against Japanese shipping in Balikpapan Harbour, Borneo. The Privateer served with the Navy until 1954 and was used to support the US Marine night attacks in Korea. They were modified to carry up to 250 lbs. high-intensity parachute-flares. These aircraft were code named 'Lamp Lighter' or 'Firefly'.

A number were used for ELINT operations with a crew of 13, one being shot down over the Baltic by a Soviet fighter in April 1950. Others were converted as the PB4Y-2M for meteorological research with all turrets

US Navy Privateer.

removed and a B-24D transparent nose section installed. The PB4Y-P was the photographic-reconnaissance version and it operated until 1955. The PB4Y-2S with additional anti-submarine radar, and the PB4Y-2K target drone were conversions. In June 1951 all surviving aircraft were re-designated as the PB4Y-2 and in 1962 as the QPB4Y-2 as ferry aircraft.

Nine were modified to become PB4Y-2Gs for use by the US Coast Guard squadrons, a number of which were converted to the bomber role. The Chinese Nationalist Air Force had the Privateer, as did Honduras with three examples. A number were converted to the AR-29 specification for fire fighting operations and were known as Super Privateers.

The Model 101 was a transport variant with a crew of four and 28 passengers. As a cargo carrier it had a hinged nose to accommodate large loads. The US Navy ordered 112 in March 1944 as the RY-3 but only 34 were delivered, the remainder cancelled.

The RAF received 26 as the Liberator C.IX, the US designation being C-87C. Finally the French navy used the Privateer extensively in Vietnam and were painted a Royal Blue overall with White lettering.

Liberator C-87, 439299 USAAF

Leading particulars B-24C

Wing span: 110ft 0in., area; 1,048 sq.ft. Length: 66ft 4ins. Height: 18ft 0in. Weights: tare; 32,330 lbs, gross; 41,000 lbs, max: 53,700 lbs. Max speed: 313mph @ 25,000ft, cruise; 233mph, landing; 93 mph. Ceiling: 34,000ft. Time-to-height: 10,000ft in 6 mins. Range: 2,100 miles with 5,000 lbs bomb load. Max; 3,600 miles. Engines: four x Pratt & Whitney R-1830 of 1,300hp @ 25,500ft. Fuel: 2,364 to 3,164 gallons. Contract dated 12 September 1940 for nine aircraft, serials 40-2378 to 2386. San Diego plant.

B-24D-160-CO, 27843, if the 376th Bombardment Group, 512th Squadron, 9th Air Force, Western Desert

Contract particulars B-24D

Contract 12464 of April 26, 1939, for six aircraft, serials 40-696 to 701. Contract 13281 of September 12, 1939, for 76 aircraft, serial 40-2349 to 2368, 41-1087 to 1142. Contract 16005 of Sept. 18, 1940, for 305 aircraft, serials 41-11587 to 11938. Eight as B-24-CF, serials. 41- 11678 as XB-24J. 41-11653 as XF-7A. Contract DA-4 of May 12, 1941, for 629 aircraft, serials 41-23640 to 24339. -43 as PB4Y-1. Contract 24620 of Feb. 19, 1942, for 1,200 aircraft, serials 42-40058 to 41257. 42-40234 as XB-24K. 44-40344 as XB-24P. 182 as PB4Y-1. Contract 30461 of June 29, 1942, for 190 aircraft, serials 42-72765 to 72963. 26 at PB4Y-1. San Diego plant.

B-24H, 44th Bombardment Group, 8th Air Force, ETO.

Leading particulars B-24H

Wing span: 110ft 0in, area; 1,048 sq.ft. Length: 67ft 2ins. Height: 18ft 0in. Weights: tare; 36,500 lbs, gross; 36,500 lbs, max; 65,000 lbs. Max speed: 290mph @ 25,000ft, cruise; 215mph, landing; 95mph. Ceiling: 28,000ft. Time-to-height: 25,000ft in 25mins. Range: 2,100 miles, 5000 lb bombs. Max range: 3,700 miles. Engines: four x Pratt & Whitney R-1850-65 of 1,200-hp @ 25,000ft. Fuel: 2,814 to 3,516 gallons.

B-24J of No. 23 Squadron RAAF

Leading particulars B-24J

Wing span: 110ft 0in., area; 1,048sq.ft, chord; (MA) 14ft. 0in. Length: 67ft 2ins. Height: 18ft 0in. Tailplane span: 26ft 0in Wheel tread: 25ft 7in. Weights: tare; 38,300 lbs, gross; 56,000lbs., max; 65,000 to 71,200lbs. Max speed: 300mph @ 30,000ft, cruise; 213mph, landing; 95mph. Combat speed: 180/215mph. Ceiling: 28,000ft, climb to 20,000ft. in 29mins. Range: 2,000 miles @ 215mph with 5,000lbs bombs @ 20,000ft. Max range: 3,000 miles. Engine: four x P&W R-1830-65 of 1,200-hp @ T/O 1,350-hp @ 30,000ft. Propeller: Hamilton Standard Hydromatic, three blade F/F. Diameter; 11ft. 7ins. Fuel: 2,364 gallons internal, 450 in auxiliary wing tanks, 800 in auxiliary bomb bay (ferry). Armament: ten x 0.50in. machine guns and 8,800lbs. bombs.

B-24M, 461st Bombardment Group, 756th Squadron, 15th Air Force, Italy.

Leading particulars. B-24M

Dimensions as for B-24H. Weights: tare; 36,000 lbs. gross; 56,000, max; 64,500. Max speed: 300mph @ 30,000ft, cruise; 215mph, landing; 95mph. Ceiling: 28,000ft, climb to 20,000ft in 25mins. Range 2100 miles with 5000 lbs. bombs, 3700 miles max. Engines: four x P&W R-1830-65 of 1200hp @ 25,000ft. Fuel: 2814 to 3614 (ferry) gallons.

Leading particulars XB-24N

Wing span: 110ft 0in, area; 1,048 sq.ft. Length: 67ft 2ins. Weights: tare; 38,300 lbs. gross; 56,000 lbs. max; 65,000 lbs. Max speed: 294mph @ 30,000ft, cruise; 213mph, landing; 95mph. Ceiling: 28,000ft. Time-to-height: 20,000ft in 29mins. Range: 2,000 miles, 5,000 lbs. bombs, max; 3,500 miles. Engines: four x P&W R-1830-75 of 1,350 hp @ 30,000ft Fuel: 2,814 to 3,614 gallons.

GR.Mk.VI Coastal Command

Leading particulars GR.VI

Wing span: 110ft 0in, area; 1048 sq.ft. Length: 67ft 11ins. Height: 17ft 11ins. Weights: tare; 37,000 lbs. gross; 62,000 lbs.. Max speed: 270mph @ 20,000ft. Time-to-height: 21,000ft in 40 mins. Range: 990 miles with 12,000 lbs. bombs, max; 2290 miles with reduced load. Ceiling: 32,000ft. Engines: four x P&W R-1830-43 Twin Wasp of 1200hp or R-1830-65 as S4Cd-G. Armament: Ten x 0.50in machine guns in nose, dorsal, tail, ventral and waist positions. Max bombs: 12,800 lbs.

Parachute conversion of C-87, Chinese Forces. Yannanyi Air Base.

Leading particulars C-87

Wing span: 110ft 0in, area; 1048sq.ft. Length: 66ft 4ins. Height: 18ft 0in. Weights: tare; 31,395 lbs. gross; 56,000 lbs.. Max speed: 306mph, cruise; 215 mph. Ceiling: 31,000ft. Time-to-height: 20,000ft in 20mins. 9secs. Range: 2900 miles. Armament: one x 0.50in machine gun.

Liberator C-109 Tanker conversion of B-24J. Burma.

US Navy RY-3 28-36 passenger transport. Note shape of engine nacelles.

CHAPTER FOUR

The Liberator in Service

The air war, as fought by the USAAF and its ally, RAF Bomber Command, was horrendous in terms of men and machines that were lost in any of the battles with the two major enemies, Germany and Japan. No quarter was given or mercy shown by either side and it was a fight, literally, to the death.

If it were possible to disassociate the suffering of modern air warfare, the whole concept and enactment of, in particular, the American daylight bombing offensive against enemy occupied Europe in World War Two would represent one of history's most prodigious spectacles of grandeur. Those long years between 1942 and 1945 represented a whole lifetime of supreme endeavour, courage and agony to an army of airmen flying and fighting far from home in a conflict that many Americans considered was not of their choosing.

They were enacting a scene in the history of the world the like of which had been undreamed of when the war started, and, hopefully, will never be known again. For those men, who crewed the Fortresses and Liberators out of England in great armadas high above the clouds of Hitler's *Festung Europa*, it was, without any doubt, the manifestation of a hitherto untried policy of daylight pin-point attacks on vital military targets. By contrast, although by mutual agreement with the United States Supreme Command, RAF Bomber Command adopted a mass bombing technique at night. These joint acts of attrition on the German military and civil installations, as well as the general population, although now with hindsight condemned, certainly hastened the enemy's collapse and final defeat.

Those great phalanxes of powerful bombers, each bristling with heavy machine-guns to be used for mutual protection against the swarms of

German interceptors, fought one of the most expensive battles both in the terms of high-technology aircraft, and the hundreds of lives of the young aviators of both opposing factions.

The United States Army Air Force's (USAAF) model of aerial bombing involving heavily armed bombers fighting their way in broad daylight to a target in mass formations was epitomised by the B-17 and B-24. Like the Spitfire and Mustang these aircraft have become legend with a assured place in world history, possibly to the exclusion of other deserving types if the criterion is their contribution to the victorious outcome of World War Two by all Allied forces.

While the USAAF continued to throw their mass formations of bombers against Germany in daylight raids, there was no denying the terror generated by the Royal Air Force Bomber Command's nocturnal activities. That Command launched its sinister black Lancaster and

B-24 Formating Monitor, 466th Bombardment, 8th Air Force, ETO.

Halifax bombers under the cloak of darkness and, as these bomber streams flew to targets illuminated by the Pathfinders, they then came under the command of the Master Bombers. When they turned for home the nimble Mosquitoes flew nuisance raids all night forcing the German civil population to spend long hours in their shelters. The USAAF's B-17s and B-24s fought their battles without the need of concealment.

The huge losses suffered, in particular by the 8th US Air Force based in England, were not in vain as its commanders absorbed the lessons of the battles over Germany, and used them to great effect in the Pacific War

B-24D with modified nose ball turret.

Theatre. The 20th US Air Force's B-29 Super Bomber employed carpet bombing to burn Japan's cities following Bomber Command's example. The lesson was clear and harsh, deprive the civil population of the will to fight and the military control will collapse. It was the Commanding Officer of Bomber Command, Air Chief Marshal 'Bomber' Harris, who had chosen that method of attack rather than attempt to only destroy military targets.

Again, in hindsight, these methods, in many instances, proved to be wrong. As with the British population, when the Luftwaffe attempted to destroy English cities during their long *Blitz* period, so the Allies' carpet-bombing of German cities and industry only strengthened their citizens resolve. The Japanese population refused to be beaten by the 'Fire raids' and it was only the horrific destruction caused by the dropping of the atomic bombs on Hiroshima and Nagasaki that brought an end to the war.

In 1942 Liberators of the 98th Bombardment Group arrived in Palestine, near Haifa and by 1 November the 1st Provisional Group had become part of the 376th Bombardment Group which was the first to operate the Liberator in Desert Pink camouflage. By the time the *Afrika Korps* had been defeated General Brereton was authorised to activate the 9th Air Force.

At the same time that Operation *Torch* was taking place Major General James Doolittle commanded the 12th US Air Force, consisting of approximately 1,250 aircraft of all types for the North African campaign. In December 1942 General Spaatz was appointed to co-ordinate the Eastern Air Command and the 12th Air Force. A single, unified Air Command was agreed in the third week of February 1943 consisting of the Mediterranean Air Forces, Eastern Air Command, 12th Air Force and ancillary units.

B-24D, 93rd Bombardment Group, 2nd Bomb Division, 8th Air Force, ETO. November 24, 1944.

The idea of creating a Strategic Air Force for the Mediterranean in Southern Italy was proposed in order that the force could easily reach and bomb targets in Austria, Germany and Eastern Europe. This plan was adopted and on November 1, the 15th Air Force was created with a strength of 90 B-24s and 210 B-17s. By the end of the month a further 201 Liberators were transferred to the new force. Fresh Groups, equipped mainly with the B-24, arrived directly from America and May 1943/44 when 13 new Liberator Groups had joined the 15th Air Force.

Between October 1, 1943, and May 1945 Liberators and Fortresses struck at targets in Germany and other occupied countries such as

B-24D, 376th Bombardment Group, 9th Air Force, Libya, in desert camouflage pink overall.

Rumania and Poland, both of which had worthwhile targets. One of the many successful operations was *Argument*, a series of heavy daylight attacks made by the 15th Air Force and supplemented by the bombers of RAF Bomber Command during the hours of darkness. This was an attempt to halt, or at least delay, production in the German aircraft industry.

Operation *Big Week* started on February 19, 1944, when the first of many attacks against German targets took place. For seven days, the 8th to the 15th, the USAAF concentrated on German industry. General Arnold stated that *Big Week* was one of the most decisive battles of history. The USAAF flew 3,000 sorties during the period with the Americans losing 244 bombers and Bomber Command and an equal amount.

When operations were halted on February 26 the American Air Force claimed they had destroyed 692 German fighters. This appears to be an improbable high number to give credence to as, during the mêlée of the

B-24D Formating Monitor, 93rd Bombardment Group, Hardwick, Norfolk, March 1944

battles that took place, many of the escorting American fighters, and bomber gunners, often claimed credit for shooting down the same fighter.

American losses, great as they were, represented only three percent of the total number of aircraft taking part. More positively for the Allies an enormous strain was put on Luftwaffe fighter pilots affecting their efforts to protect their homeland. As more pilots were sucked into the air battles so the Luftwaffe found it more difficult to replace them with men possessing skill and experience.

Mission Into Germany

The ferocity with which the Luftwaffe fought the Allied bombers as they stepped up their attacks against targets in mainland Germany can be

Crew man holds parachute lines that slowed this B-24H during landing without brakes.

appreciated by this account of one large bombing raid made by the Eighth Air Force during an attack against a target on the German-Austrian border.

The defence put up by the Germans was one of the stiffest ever met by the bomber force of the Liberators and Fortresses plus their escorts which had to fight their way through to the target for almost two hours. The official report compiled from stories from the actual bomber crews provides virtually the complete report of the German fighters the bombers met and the tactics they employed by them in one of the fiercest battles fought up to that that by the 8th Air Force aircraft.

Republic P-47 Thunderbolts and Spitfire F.Mk.XIVs escorted the bomber force for the first section of their long penetration into Germany. From the beginning, as the bombers crossed the Channel coast, there was heavy, and persistent, interception by the Luftwaffe from a point twenty miles south-east of Brussels, in Belgium to approximately 30 miles east of the target. German fighters attacked in relays of from 20 to 30 fighters every few minutes.

Initially there was little flak (Ack-Ack fire) but soon after the American force had crossed the Belgian coast a huge formation of 200 or more enemy fighters attacked. Many of the bomber crews reported occasional short attacks by the Luftwaffe until just after the escorting fighters had turned back having reached the end of their range. As the bombers flew deeper into Germany so they were met with a veritable storm of fighters, and the deeper they drove into German air space the heavier the attacks developed. There were a variety of types of enemy fighters, included a large percentage of Messerschmitt Bf 109Gs, Focke-Wulf Fw 190s, Messerschmitt 110s, 210s and 410s, Junkers Ju 88 fighters, Dornier Do 217s and Focke-Wulf 189s with packs of machine-guns hung under the forward fuselage.

The fighter force kept being replenished and appeared to be inexhaustible and all known Luftwaffe tactics were witnessed with attacks from all directions and angles. The majority of attacks were by groups of fighters approaching simultaneously from two, six and ten o'clock, and bomber crews reported that in many instances they also attacked from high altitude, targeting the high squadrons and then diving through the formations. Frontal attacks were made from slightly above in addition to from below, and the majority of individual attacks were made from out of the sun.

A number of bomber crews stated that one or more Luftwaffe fighters flew alongside the Fortresses and Liberators acting as decoys for the American gunners to concentrate on at the same time as other fighters attacked from the nose and tail positions. One pilot flying in the rear group of bombers described how the German fighters flew into the squadrons and attacked the Group ahead and were seen to have shot down one Fortress and damaging a second.

The final group of bombers also encountered the second attack wave and the No. 2 Fortress went spiralling down in flames. In the following attack Fortress No. 3 went down and, in another attack wave, the leading Fortress of the second element went down as the pilot of the following bomber saw strikes on his No. 3 engine while a 20-mm cannon shell exploded in the nose section. However, the aircraft managed to maintain his formation position. The tail-gunners were almost continuously in action with attacks being made by groups of fighters coming in, six at a time, from all directions. This type of attack was frowned upon by the Luftwaffe as, inevitably, the attacking fighter proved to be vulnerable.

One crew-member of a Fortress saw a Me Bf 109 following his bomber

B-24J, 491st Bombardment Group, 8th Air Force, bombing Germany, May 4, 1945.

and keeping out of range, not attacking. He considered the enemy fighter pilot was sending warning of the bomber's speed, course and height. As the bombers flew on towards their target they could see reinforcement German fighters climbing to join in the battle at the same moment as the others landed to refuel and re-arm. One gunner witnessed seven fighters at 11 o'clock, six at ten, five at three and three at 9 o'clock. They all appeared to come in at the same moment and circled round to then dash into the formation. Groups of 15 or more would attack a single bomber and there would be sudden bursts of activity when fighter packs of up to 75 aircraft would sweep in to be followed by the same number when the first pack peeled away. It was obvious the fighters were attacking to an agreed plan or were being controlled by master fighters in the air.

*B-24J drops shower of 'fragment' bombs on Neugburg airfield, Austria, a Luftwaffe base.
460th Bombardment Group.*

The bombers battled their way through the enemy fighter forces for an
hour or more and to the bomber crews it appeared to be a lifetime. The
top turret gunner of one Fortress watched as hordes of fighters climbed
over the bombers to attack at their leisure and were thought to be
controlled by a high circling Me 110 twin engined fighter. One
bombardier witnessed hordes of fighters flying wing tip to wing tip, in
groups of six, and four or more of these groups would attack as one
formation.

Some Me Bf 109s were reported to be firing heavy cannon carried
under the fighter's wings, probably the Naxos pack, the shell explosions

B-24J flies over the Alps en route to bomb Austria.

resembling heavy flak. A waist gunner stated he saw Ju 88s and Me 110s firing what appeared to be heavy 37mm shells, some of which overshot and exploded ahead of his bomber. Several enemy fighters were seen to

B-24Js, 460th Bomb Group, 15th Air Force, after bombing Gmund rail yards, Austria.

be firing rockets from under-wing installations and other witnesses watched as some enemy fighters flew ahead of the formation to climb sharply and drop clusters of 20 to 30 brown objects that passed in towards and into the formation before exploding.

The Luftwaffe fighters maintained the weight of their attacks for two hours in running battles and these stopped before the target was reached. The attacks suddenly stopped for no apparent reason leaving the bombers a clear run over the target. After bombing the bomber formation flew on to North Africa, and once they left the target the fighter attacks were sporadic, but bombers that were damaged and straggled behind the main force were quickly despatched by the Germans.

Regensburg and Schweinfurt

Fleets of B-17s and B-24s flew by day with the RAF supporting their actions at night. The most well known raids that the 15th US Air Force took part in were on the Messerschmitt factories at Regensburg with the 8th Air Force striking the ball-bearing works at Schweinfurt. The 15th Air Force attacked Obertraubling but as the force of 118 B-24s approached the target the Luftwaffe was ready and waiting, having concentrated a large fighter force there. However, despite all their efforts they shot down a relatively low total of 14 aircraft.

The Regensburg-Schweinfurt operation was a test of the effectiveness of the German fighter defence system and the plans called for the Liberators and Fortresses to penetrate 200 miles into Germany to reach Schweinfurt and another 200 further to Regensburg. The later formations would avoid the hazards of a return trip across Germany by flying to bases in Algeria. By flying immediately after the Regensburg force the Schweinfurt bomber crews had hoped for a comparatively clear path as much of the German fighter force would have been committed against the earlier mission.

The Messerschmitt works at Regensburg and Wiener Neustadt produced nearly half of Germany's single engined fighters and, in Schweinfurt, half of the German ball-bearing output. The 8th Air Force commanders considered that bombing the factories would significantly affect Germany's war effort.

The Regensburg force of 146 bombers left England on the morning of the August 17, 1943, and on reaching the borders of Germany were attacked by a swarm of enemy fighters for an hour and a half. Fighters from as far away from the Baltic were directed to the scene and spotters flew just out of range to instruct the waiting fighters when and where to attack. Twenty-four bombers were destroyed, the majority before

Plan view of 467th Bombardment Group, 8th Air Force Liberator over Snabrook, Germany, March 23,1945.

reaching the target, but as the bombers neared Regensburg the fighter attack slackened enabling the Americans a good bombing run.

On the return trip the bombers crossed the Alps and proceeded to landing grounds in Africa. The Schweinfurt bombers were delayed from take-off for almost four hours and by the time they had reached Germany the fighter force had been refuelled and rearmed and was waiting. The fighter attacks were more ferocious both to and from the target and did not slacken until the American force staggered across the Channel. A total of 230 bombers were despatched; 36 were destroyed, and many more

B-24 of the 15th Air Force was hit by AA fire while attacking Munich rail yards. Petrol tanks are ablaze.

damaged or crashed on landing. The raid would have been considered Pyrrhic if measured in terms of a single battle, but in the overall scheme of bombing attacks it showed the bombers were successfully hitting their targets and wearing down the German fighter force.

A second Schweinfurt attack further highlighted the danger of sending unescorted bombers across Germany. Of the 291 bombers despatched 60 were destroyed for the cost of 35 German fighters. The Germans attacked in waves from all angles, a number of the defending Me 210s firing rockets from the rear, normally concentrating on a single formation of bombers. The Germans had learned the lessons meted out to them during the Battle of Britain.

In further raids carpets of bombs fell on factories in Brunswick, Ascherleben, Bernburg, Leipzig, Augsburg, Stuttgart, Furth, Gotha,, Tutow and Posen. Despite all this activity German industry continued to build aircraft and other war materials by moving production away from the major cities and towns and moving plants underground.

By the autumn of 1944 the average monthly figure for aircraft production alone over a period of seven months had reach 3,650 of which 2,500 were day fighters. The factories also had to be defended and Reichsmarschall Göring was forced to withdraw his fighter squadrons away from German forces defending the Atlantic Wall in Europe and the vital Eastern Front in Russia.

But in the end it was not aircraft production that the Luftwaffe lacked. During November 1944 the newly dispersed factories produced a huge total of 4,000 fighters. The problem was that they had to be able to operate and a lack of fuel and pilots kept the new aircraft on the ground. The Allied bombers were attacking oil supplies by day and by night as well as other factories, and such was the shortage of fuel that all training in the Luftwaffe was halted, a self-defeating manoeuvre as new pilots were required and they had to be able to fly their aircraft. This situation exacerbated the problem of finding suitably trained pilots to replace losses. It was, of course, not just the Luftwaffe that suffered from the lack of fuel. The armoured columns with the supply vehicles also required fuel to keep them rolling.

During the period of increased attacks against Germany a large number of fighters were concentrated on Berlin and they were needed. The number of attacks of 1943/44 saw Bomber Command alone attack the city 18 times with the USAAF attacking during the daylight hours. Neither of these included other, numerous attacks on equally important targets. The table below lists details of USAAF raids by Liberators and

B-24 Liberator of the 15th Air Force drops its bombs on rail yards at Krams, Austria, April 2, 1945.

Fortresses for three months – March to May 1944.

Date	Target	Force	Tonnage	US a/c Missing	Enemy a/c Claimed
Mar 6	Berlin	bombers	1,650	68	98
Mar 8	Berlin	bombers	1,073	38	42
Mar 9	Berlin	bombers	775	7	0
Mar 22	Berlin	bombers	1,430	13	0
Mar 24	Berlin	bombers	2,500	73	0
Apr 29	Berlin	bombers	1,400	63	14
May 7	Berlin	bombers	1,246	8	72
May 8	Berlin	bombers	892	36	60
May 19	Berlin	bombers	914	26	53
May 24	Berlin	bombers	1,081	32	48

It is interesting to note that as the Allies increased their daylight attacks in 1944 to prepare for the forthcoming landings in Normandy, the number

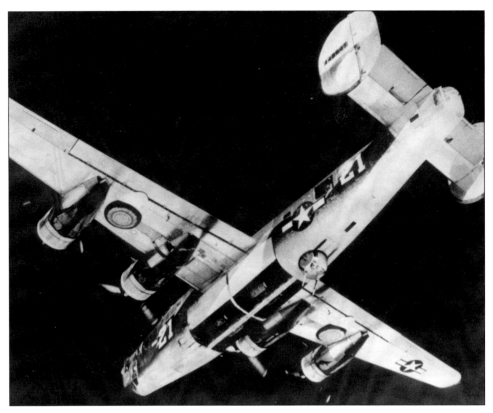

Excellent view of the B-24's bomb bays in open position. Also position of ventral turret.

of German aircraft claimed as destroyed by the bombers showed a significant increase. During the same period the Royal Air Force Lancasters and Halifaxes dropped 20,000 tons of bombs including a high

B-24D Formating Monitor, 93rd Bombardment Group, Hardwick, Norfolk, March 1944

proportion of 4,000 lbs. block-busters.

During April 1944 Air Marshal Harris, C-in-C Bomber Command, launched his forces against German sources of liquid, natural and synthetic fuel. Germany was being denied the opportunity to keep its military machine operating. The Luftwaffe could not adequately defend the Third Reich.

In that month bomber forces were also used on other energy producing factories, striking at plants in Leuna, Bohlen, Zeitz, Lutzkendorf and Brux. During the following month two attacks by American bombers laid waste to the huge hydrogenation plants at Politz and Pomerania.

Eight saturation raids were made against Berlin between November 1943 and March 1944 when a staggering 30,000 tons of bombs were dropped on the city. On these statistics both the RAF and USAAF calculated that a total of approximately 90,000 to 100,000 tons of bombs would have to be dropped to ensure complete destruction of the city. Even the combined forces of the Allies could not be massed to complete this task without stripping other fronts of bombers.

It would have required a total of 40,000 to 50,000 raids with contemporary medium bombers (not the B-29) travelling 60,000,000 miles and consuming approximately 15,000,000 gallons of fuel. No bomber force could ever hope to meet this enormous task, disproving the Bomber Baron's statements that their Air Forces alone could win the war.

Some attacks did produce startling results, such as the daylight raid by the USAAF on the important Focke-Wulf main assembly factory at Bremen on April 17, 1943. The whole area was heavily damaged to the extent that at the Germans evacuated the factory equipment and employees to Marienburg, a small town on the Pomeranian-Polish border.

B-24D Formating Monitor, 44th Bombardment Group, 8th Air Force, ETO.

The Allies were aware of the move by means of reconnaissance flights and when the factory had been re-established it was attacked again, this time destroying 70 percent of all the buildings.

The factory was rebuilt and once again the Americans reduced it to rubble on April 9, 1944. During the period of the raids, spread over three days, the Americans lost 76 bombers and fighters. In return they claimed to have shot down 217 Luftwaffe fighters.

Between January 1943 and December 1943 Allied Air Forces dropped no less than 135,000 tons of bombs upon German targets. The German defences had to be increased and this could only take place at the expense of withdrawing forces from the Russian front, depriving it of men and materials.

The USAAC's 8th Air Force launched more than 1,000 B-17s and B-24s against Berlin's railway system on June 21, 1944. A total of 1,300 tons of bombs were dropped and in a few, short minutes, it was all over. Between July 1943 and July 1944 bombers of the USAAF's 8th and 15th Air Force fought the enemy to a standstill over Germany and Austria.

So far as the Allies were concerned the combined resources of America and Britain accounted for 86,000 aircraft of all types produced between 1942 and 1943, the British contribution being 28,000 consisting of 4,614

B-24J 'Cuddles'. 460th Bombardment Group. Non standard fin markings.

heavy bombers (Lancaster/Halifax) and 10,727 fighters and other types. For Operation *Overlord*, the invasion of Europe, the Germans were in the unenviable position of facing an Allied armada of 3,467 heavy bombers, 1,645 medium bombers and 5,400 fighter and attack aircraft. Facing this total the Luftwaffe could deploy just 429 aircraft.

For *Overlord* a systematic attack on German communications was launched and such was the combined strength of the American and British Air Forces that sufficient aircraft were readily available. Allied forces started attacking along the River Seine between Rouen and Paris after the breakout from Normandy, with similar attacks along the Albert Canal from Antwerp to Liege, ending at Namur. In these areas a total of twenty principal railway junctions were totally destroyed. By this method Eisenhower attempted to prevent the German 15th Army from intervening on the left bank of the Seine.

Also, Army Group G, with its eight divisions stationed between Nantes and Hendave, Perignan and Menton, was subjected to many air attacks in the area through which it had to move in order to prevent any major Allied attack. Bridges over the Seine were destroyed for the same reason. Attacks on railway traffic were so intense that by July 6, 1943, movement had been halved.

Attacks on coastal and heavy gun emplacements followed between Cape Gris-Nez and Cape Barfluer, and many gun batteries between Le Havre and Cherbourg. Such was the destruction from the air that the

B-24J, 389th Bombardment Group, 8th Air Force, ETO. 'The Shack'.

Germans were forced to move a great number of troops from the immediate area of the coast and relocate them further inland, and that was the Allied intention.

European operations by Liberators

An interesting facet of the early American bombing campaign in Europe was the use of a 'Pathfinder Force', pioneered by the Royal Air Force. Cloudy and overcast conditions were almost the norm over Europe and the USAAF was frustrated by the many delays to operations. The RAF, who used the 'Gee' navigational device, made this technology available to the Americans.

In late 1942 8th Air Force Liberators experimented with 'Gee' in daylight 'Moling' (Intruder) flights over Germany with sorties of single aircraft, their main purpose being to disrupt operations by the Luftwaffe and to suspend output from the factories which, normally, stopped when the alarm was sounded. These operations were suspended in March 1943 but not before the American Pathfinders had completely absorbed the technology.

Other navigational aids made available to the USAAF by Britain were the H2S and the 'Oboe', the former being an airborne scanner that provided a rough electronic map, of the terrain the bomber was flying

B-24H, 451st Bomb Group, 15th Air Force, is hit by Fw 190 fighter during attack on Focke-Wulf factory at Markensdorf, 20 August 1944.

over, on a cathode ray tube. The USAAF formed a special group to experiment with the apparatus in August 1943 with the 482nd (Pathfinder) Group stationed at Alconbury, with one Liberator and two B-17 squadrons.

The training of the Pathfinder crews took place with British smoke marker bombs, guided by H2S, being dropped at a given point by formation leaders, indicating the correct aiming point. The American produced sets were called AN/APS-15 'Mickey' units and pathfinder

B-24H 'Final Approach' takes off.

units were to be established in three Air Divisions.

The first attack was against five aircraft manufacturing plants in the Brunswick area of Germany, with the 482nd providing Liberator Pathfinders. The weather closed in over the target and the Second and Third Air Divisions recalled their fighters and bombers. However, the first Air Division continued with the raid with the eventual loss of 34 aircraft, one of which was equipped with H2S.

A new technique had obviously to be formulated and the result was the HEX Synchronous Bombing Tactic, led by the 482nd Pathfinders and used in the attacks against German ground forces in the Normandy area. Thus the Allied forces were able to advance against the German troops with the bombs being dropped a mere 800 yards ahead of the advance guard. The USAAF also adopted HEX, AN/APQ-7, Rececca (SCR-799), AN/APS 13, 'Gee', 'Gee-H', Loran and RCM.

Clandestine operations were carried out, during the final stages of the war, by converted Liberators with all military gear removed and closely fitted seats installed. They were to be used for operations carrying ground personnel between Sweden and England. In 1944 a large number of

B-14H, 458th Bombardment Group, 8th Air Force. 'Gas House Mouse'.

Norwegians escaped across the border into Sweden and took part in military training using Swedish Instructors. The Norwegian Government in England asked the British and American Governments to air lift the newly trained troops to Britain to form an army and to transport them into Norway prior to the Normandy landings.

It was agreed, with the aid of the Swedish Government, that the converted Liberators were to be flown by American and British crews. The aircraft had all military markings removed, and crews from the 93rd Bombardment Group and 389th flew five C-7 Liberators. However, the Germans had been made aware of the operations and alerted fighter patrols along the Swedish border from Norway where approximately 200 German fighters were stationed.

The first operation took place in April 1944 when 40 Norwegians were airlifted to England. Any German fighters were picked up by British radar and the transports diverted. During the period from March to December 1944, 110 round trips were made and eventually 1,847 Norwegian trainees and 965 Americans were brought back to the UK, to the annoyance of the Germans. The same Liberators were used to supply Norwegian Resistance movements with Sten machine guns, ammunition, explosives, food and clothing. Eventually there was a force of six Liberators being used for these operations under the code name of 'Carpetbaggers'.

Turning attention to France the Allies' Operation *Anvil*, the softening up of targets in the area, was launched and the towns of Marseilles, Lyon, Grenoble and Toulon were heavily bombed. Throughout the summer of 1944 aircraft factories in Austria felt the weight of the US 15th Air Force onslaught. Additionally whole fleets of B-24s and B-17s, now with P-51 Mustang escort fighters, attacked many oil targets.

When the first German jet fighter, the Me 262, twin-jet aircraft appeared, the Allies could only respond with the Gloster Meteor but it is not known if these two jet fighters ever met in combat. American response to the

B-24Hs of the 458th Bombardment Group, running up at Horsham St Faith. February 26, 1945.

threat was swift and decisive. On March 21, 366 B-24s attacked the Messerschmitt factory and airfield at Neugerb and the plant was virtually destroyed. Three days later a second, heavy strike, by 271 Liberators completed the destruction.

Just before the war ended the 15th Air Force launched what was the heaviest raid of that campaign when 1,235 bombers attacked Wowser, near Bologna, Italy. By the time the war had ended, during 18 months of fighting the 15th Air Force had dropped 304,000 tons of bombs on targets in 12 countries, a large proportion of those targets being oil installations. However, the cost had been high with the 8th, 9th, 12th and 15th Air Forces losing some 1,756 Liberators between them.

C-109 Liberator.

'Marco Polo' was a transport conversion of the Liberator. AL578 serial number.

XB-24J fitted with B-17G transparent nose.

Unusual designation of EZB-24 of Aero Icing Research Laboratory.

This B-24 had a ball ventral gun turret.

CHAPTER FIVE

The Oil Targets

Ploesti in Rumania was just one important target in a whole series of attacks on the German oil industry, the 15th US Air Force having targeted over 870 refineries.

The raids on Ploesti started on June 11, 1942, when a force of 13 Liberators of the USAAC's 10th Air Force took off from the RAF Fayed airfield in Egypt. The 10th Air Force usually operated from bases in India and the Far East but a detachment of 23 B-24Ds, commanded by Colonel H A Halverson, and originally intended for bomber operations on Japan from bases in China, were given the task. The detachment, initially held over in Egypt on a temporary basis for this mission, was eventually absorbed into the 9th US Air Force. All night, across the Mediterranean, the Aegean, Greece and Bulgaria, the Liberators flew unmolested to the Ploesti oilfields. They arrived at dawn on the 12th, in squadron order, after a flight of 1,400 miles and, due to the unlikely direction they took, encountered very little opposition. The Liberator force carried a relatively small bomb load of about 4,000 lbs. per aircraft and, through cloud at approximately 10,000ft, they managed to hit the Astra Refinery as well as other targets. After the raid finished and the bombers had left the area, they had to land in whatever country they could. Seven aircraft managed to land at the RAF base at Habbaniya in Iraq, two landed in Syria and the remaining four landed in neutral Turkey where the crews were interned and the aircraft taken over by the Turkish Air Force. All in all it was an inauspicious start to the Oil Campaign and served to alert the Axis powers to the threat of future attacks from southern bases.

The B-24s were painted in a Desert Pink overall (see colour pages) and continued their operations in the Mediterranean seeking out Rommel's

B-24Ds fly low over Ploesti oil fields.

reinforcement shipping convoys, and in the Western Desert against the *Afrika Korps*. When Rommel was defeated the British 8th Army swept forward from El Alamein and drove towards Tunisia.

Reinforcement of the Luftwaffe in North Africa, during the final months of the *Afrika Korps'* resistance in Tunisia, resulted in the despatch of a single, fragmented *Gruppe* of Focke-Wulf Fw 190A-4/Trop. fighters to bolster *Fliegerführer Tunis*. Surviving records suggest that these aircraft achieved a measure of success against the American P-38 Lightnings, but most met their end on the ground when caught by raiding allied twin-engine medium bombers, such as the B-26 Marauder.

Sixty-eight 190A-4/Tropical sand-filter equipped fighters were built, the majority with a fighter-bomber rack capable of carrying a single SC250 (550 lbs) bomb. The surviving Focke-Wulfs were evacuated to Sicily, each pilot frequently carrying one, or even two, ground crewmen squeezed into the rear cockpit or in the radio compartment.

With the collapse of Axis Forces in North Africa in 1943, II, III and IV *Gruppen*, SKG10 (*Schnelles Kampfgeschwader* or fast-bomber), under the command of *Major* Temme, were hurriedly transferred to Sicily to counter the invasion of that island. They proved, however, to be of little value in the face of overwhelming allied air superiority.

German and Italian forces in Sicily clashed with the allied forces landing troops on the island. And the Fw 190s were flung into battle as the enemy troops could only fight to contain the invasion against a mass of men and machines of the landing force. The fortunes of the Luftwaffe faired no better during the Sicilian campaign and the tattered remnants of

SKG10's fighter-bombers were forced to disperse among the airfields and emergency grounds around Gerbini.

They made many abortive attacks against allied shipping and ground installations in the south of the island after July 10, 1943, but were constantly harried by the Lightnings and Spitfires. Once again the Germans retreated, this time to the Italian mainland leaving their Italian allies to fight on alone for the island. The end came in Italy after a long, hard slog and the almost extinction of *Feldmarschall* Kesselring's *Luftlotte* 2 in 1944.

Allied battleships and bombers, including the Liberators pounded enemy defences and their aircraft, and made it almost impossible for the Luftwaffe fighters to get into the air in sufficient numbers to make any difference to the allied advance.

While this battle was proceeding attention was turned once again to the oil targets with Ploesti high on the list. On June 20, 1943, training, using a full-scale mock-up of Ploesti, was laid out in the desert sands. Dire consequences were predicted with a high loss rate, calculated at 50 percent of the raiders shot down to, from and over, the target. When the mission was finally announced for August 1, 1943, the B-24 crews were noticeably apprehensive.

The 2nd Bombardment Wing of the 8th Air Force provided two Liberator units, the 44th and the 93rd Bombardment Groups which, after special low-level training in England, were sent to Benghazi in Libya where they joined the 98th and 376th Bombardment Groups of the 9th Air Force. These two groups were strengthened by the arrival of a new bombardment unit, the 389th which had also arrived from England. After further training, 177 Liberators from the five groups took off from Benghazi on August 1, 1943, for the 2,700 miles return flight. The 376th Bombardment Group, led the Liberator force, to be followed by the 93rd, the 98th and the 44th, with the 389th in the rear. The bombers all carried 500 lbs. bombs and an additional 400 gallons of fuel in the bomb-bay. The B-24s headed out over the Mediterranean to turn east over Corfu and proceed into Southern Europe. The first Liberators reached the oilfields at approximately 14.00 hours and that is when the first error occurred.

The lead group, the 376th, had overshot the IP and turned south to be followed by the 93rd to Bucharest, where they met with extensive flak. In the meantime the 389th had turned to the correct position and, finding the oil field defences relatively light, blasted the Campire Refinery. The force split into two, and the aircraft that had flown over Bucharest turned towards the target only to be met, with dire results, by a now alerted

B-24H flies over Hamburg to bomb Shulan oil refinery. 489th Bombardment Group, 8th Air Force.

defence. Nine aircraft were immediately shot down and of the 177 B-24s that had taken part in the attack 57 failed to return, over 30% of the entire force. The remaining aircraft were forced to land in various places throughout the Middle East and remained ineffective as a fighting force for some considerable time.

The raid appeared to be a waste of men and machines as Ploesti, following this attack, was in full production within four weeks. However, on April 5, 1944, the USAAF were again to despatch a force of 236 Liberators and Fortresses from the 15th Air Force to Ploesti, and other similar attacks followed until the supply of fuel from the refineries was finally reduced to a mere trickle.

This ex PB4Y-2 has been fitted with the B-25 Mitchell engine/nacelles.

PB4Y-2 Privateer.

PB4Y-1 Chinese Nationalist Air Force.

N9860C of US Navy with unusual dorsal fitting.

PB4Y-2 in overall Navy Blue. ATU 600

CHAPTER SIX

The Battle of the Atlantic

The Battle of the Atlantic was the dominating factor all through the war. "Never forget for one moment that everything elsewhere depended upon its outcome." These were the words spoken by Winston Churchill during World War Two when victory for the Allies appeared certain.

For the allies the Battle of the Atlantic was not only a race to develop new and advanced weapons quicker than the enemy, in particular the U-boat, it was also a race to produce anti-submarine aircraft, such as the long-range, four-engine bombers, and, of course the escort ships that could protect the merchant shipping.

Before the war an escort programme had been sadly neglected and when the allies were thrown out of France any plans that existed for this task were virtually abandoned. Priority was given to the chronic shortage of ships and aircraft, in addition to the task of re-arming the army and building up Fighter Command. The Royal Navy had to wait until the summer of 1942 when a massive building programme of destroyers, frigates and corvettes got underway, both here and in Canada – which

Group of Coastal Command Liberators.

contributed in a massive way to the build-up of the allied forces.

Coastal Command and Bomber Command began to re-equip with the aircraft they desperately needed to take the battle to the German homeland and to provide forces with which to beat the U-boat. England had battled on during the period and was just about holding off the enemy until the United States, now in the war, could start the flow of war materials. This, however, was not the difficulty; shipping the materials across the Atlantic, which was heavily infested with U-boats, was.

Within months the catastrophic effects of the U-boats' almost unhindered pursuit of Allied convoys began to be felt and Germany, believing the Allies were on the road to defeat, halted their own expansion race.

The odds were strongly in favour of the U-boat fleet in early 1941 and they lengthened further until 1942 when Allied anti-submarine forces started to take effect. Additional anti-submarine training schools were established and all the new materials in the form of ships, new armament and aircraft were going through their acceptance trials.

To add to the problems being experienced by Coastal Command the appearance of the long-range Focke-Wulf four-engined patrol bomber, which could operate up to 800 miles into the Atlantic, added yet another dimension. A number of escort carriers were eventually provided but the Admiralty could not wait for them to arrive into service and a stop-gap was required.

The new weapon introduced into the Allied arsenal against the U-boat was the 'Hedgehog', a weapon that was basically a naval version of the mortar bomb. There was also the 'Squid'. Both weapons threw their missiles ahead of the ship in a pattern designed to straddle the U-boat.

Liberator GR.VI.NF 311 (Czechoslovakia) Coastal Command, RAF

The charges dropped and exploded at different intervals and depths so as to give the maximum coverage. Twenty 'Hedgehog' bombs per volley could be launched and these would explode on contact with a U-boat's hull. The 'Squid' dropped three bombs to explode around the U-boat's hull to crack it and force the vessel to the surface, for the convoy escort ships to finish the job with gunfire.

PB4Y-1 Privateer in White and Grey paint scheme.

A new version of the Asdic transmitter-receiver was also installed on the escort vessels. This utilised sound impulses, rather than radar pulses. The sound impulses were sent out in an arc and, when it made contact with a submerged vessel the signal 'bounced' off the hull and returned. The calibration of the length of time this returned impulse took established the U-boat's position. The developed form of Asdic sent three impulses, one diffused over a wide area and two over a more narrow arc.

By 1943 the battle was at its height with the climax reached in March 1943. The German U-boat fleet of active boats was 240 with a total of 112 in the Atlantic. On the Allied side there appeared the first of the escort carriers and the arrival of additional numbers of anti-submarine aircraft. These included the Liberator and Catalina for the long-range operations, the Sunderland for the medium range and the Wellington and Warwick, plus the Hudson, for the short-range.

The war plans of the Royal Navy had been taking shape since 1936 when Hitler marched into the Rhineland without any opposition or protest from the League of Nations and that had set the pattern for further aggression by the dictator. Plans were being made in anticipation, by the navy, that war would break out in the latter part of 1939, an extremely accurate forecast.

One of the results of that forecast was a supplementary naval estimate

B-24D with highly modified nose similar to that on Coastal Command Liberators. 308th Bombardment, 14th Air Force.

by Parliament for the construction of two new battleships, an aircraft carrier, five cruisers and a number of supporting vessels. The following year the estimates included three more battleships, two more aircraft carriers, seven cruisers and a large increase in the number of smaller vessels.

The war plans drawn up by the Admiralty in January 1939 represented the adoption of a defensive strategy and was based on the assumption

B-24D in ASR colour scheme of White and Grey. Note side nose guns

that the war would be fought against Germany and Italy from the start. Three main areas were considered to be vital to England: (1) the defence of trade in home waters, (2) the Mediterranean and, (3) the Indian Ocean. It was assumed that if Italy conducted an aggressive war with its large navy it would force all trade in the area to take the longer route around the Cape of Good Hope.

The main battle fleet was concentrated in Scotland and cruisers of the Northern Patrol kept watch, waiting to intercept any enemy or neutral ship. The submarine flotillas were based at Dundee and Blyth. In the Mediterranean the French Navy would hold the western basin and, the eastern part, the British force based at Alexandria.

The German war plans for their fleet were chaotic as it was unprepared for war. But they did have available three pocket battleships, two battle cruisers and just 56 U-boats of which 46 were ready with well trained crews. The battle instructions were for the fleet to conduct a series of operations in the North Sea and tie down part of the Royal Navy, while the larger ships would cruise the ocean and attack merchant shipping. The U-boats were to operate against trade in the Atlantic. Apart from the U-boats and a number of forays by the larger ships, the German fleet was virtually inoperable and it was the U-boat that posed the largest threat.

Early consideration had been given to the need to defend Britain's lifeline to America. The Royal Navy, in planning the shape of the convoy

Consolidated PB4Y-1 on coastline patrol.

defence when the ships were crossing the ocean, had produced a plan that was based upon the knowledge gained by the U-boat attacks during the First World War. These war plans had been issued to all Royal Navy Commanders in January 1939 and they presented a defensive strategy as it was obvious that Germany would wage a sea war.

The major section was the defence of waterborne trade in home waters and the Atlantic. The plans also incorporated the requirement to ensure a steady stream of supplies from other parts of the Commonwealth.

Between August 19th and 29th, 1939, 17 U-boats were sent to the Atlantic and two of the battleships also slipped out into the Atlantic. In the first successful attack by a U-boat on a British ship, the liner Athenia was sunk by the U-boat U-30.

A further section was the defence of, and maintenance of supplies, in the Mediterranean, including the protection of Malta, Gibraltar and the Indian Ocean, although the latter was not considered urgent as the entry of Japan in to the war had not been accurately predicted. The solution was a possible blockade with, later, the Royal Navy stopping and searching all neutral shipping carrying materials to the Axis Nations. This had worked extremely well in World War One.

The year 1941 was a hard one for the merchant marine and the British nation as during that twelve months hundreds of ships were sent to the bottom of the ocean. During January and February U-boats sank 21 ships and the bombers almost equalled that with a total of 20. In February it was worse with 39 ships sunk by U-boats and 27 by the Fw 200 'Condor'. Britain was bleeding to death although the convoy system was beginning to pay dividends and the total of losses fell for a period

But the German answer to this was the establishment of the 'Wolf Pack' when numbers of U-boats, often supplied with details of the position of the allied convoys by the Fw 200, would congregate in its path and wreak destruction. When America finally entered the war the U-boats operated close to the continent's eastern coast where they sunk American ships very close to the shores.

What was desperately required was a method of 'closing the gap' between the two countries which the U-boats patrolled. It already existed in small numbers as Coastal Command had acquired 20 Liberators released to it by President Roosevelt, and they were fitted with ASV and anti-submarine weapons. Also the Royal and American navies were receiving new weapons that flushed the U-boats to the surface or destroyed them under water.

In 1941 the Allies had lost a staggering total of 432 ships to the U-boats and 371 to the Condor bomber, contributing to a total loss of 1,664 ships. The ship building programmes of the allies, England, Canada and America, could not keep pace with this amount of destruction until the American Liberty ship programme got into full production. Slowly the allies regained control of the Atlantic and began to drive the U-boats out of the oceans. The German Admiral Dönitz had calculated that by sinking 800,000 tons of Allied shipping every month Germany would win the war. That total was almost reached at the height of the battle during

B-24D Formating Monitor, 445th Bombardment Group, 8th Air Force, England.

March 1942 with a total of 650,000 tons.

Opposing the Royal Navy was a small number of capital ships and smaller craft of the German Navy including the so-called 'Pocket Battleships' and 'Hipper Class' large cruisers. The former were found to be very effective as surface raiders and the Royal Navy had a difficult task of trying to trace them in the large areas of the world's oceans.

By June 1941 Coastal Command had 40 aircraft in service, a small number of which, such as the Wellington bomber, were equipped with ASV. The aircraft carried all types of depth charges, plus other new devices particularly radar, to beat the German Navy. Even more urgently required was an aeroplane that would protect, and close, the vital Atlantic Gap.

The aircraft that ultimately fulfilled this task was the B-24 Liberator flying from both sides of the ocean and meeting in the middle. British aircraft could have been modified to carry additional fuel (Halifax and Lancaster) but they were wanted by Bomber Command. However, at the limit of their patrols these modified aircraft could not loiter as the fuel they carried was insufficient. With bases in Iceland also alleviating the situation the area of greatest danger narrowed but was not entirely closed.

There is little doubt it was the long range Liberator that made possible the closing of the Atlantic Gap where the rampaging U-boats almost brought Britain to her knees in the early years of the war. A total of 34

GR.Mk.VIII, KH228, of RAF Coastal Command. Twin Wasp engines.

aircraft could protect the British and American convoys for the first section of their journey to America. But they had to abandon the convoys to the weak cover afforded by the few Royal Navy vessels in the 'gap' before they came under the protection of aircraft and warships that were stationed in Newfoundland. The mid-Atlantic gap could not be bridged before the advent of the long-range bomber.

A further problem faced by the Allies was the Condor, Germany's long-range patrol bomber. The Admiralty tried a variety of methods to combat this menace, one being the use of an old, converted seaplane carrier, the Pegasus, modified to carry a number of fighters, such as the Hurricane. Another solution was to install a small ramp on a selected number of merchantmen that could launch a Hurricane fighter by catapult for a one way journey. The fighter could not return to the ship and the pilot had to land his aeroplane in the water as near a ship as possible in order to be picked up. It was a risky operation all round and a number of these 'Hurricat' pilots were lost on what proved to be a near suicide operation. The Condor was an extremely effective weapon for not only could it find and shadow the convoys and radio their position to the lurking U-boats, it could also attack the ships with bombs.

B-24J of the 461st Bombardment Group.

It was not until January 1942 when America was fighting the same war as Britain that any firm action could be taken to provide a long-range patrol bomber that could bridge the gap and, importantly, remain over the convoy for several vital hours. Only after 40 Allied ships had been sunk in one week did the threat really sink into the American consciousness and the 44th and 93rd Liberator Bombardment Groups were made available for anti-submarine duties.

By the end of May 1942 the U-boat was enjoying what the German commanders called 'The Happy Time', achieving a rate of 650,000 tons of Allied shipping lost per month, greater than the number of ships being produced in England.

In the meantime work had started on the development of a number of counter weapons to the U-boat and Condor, the most significant of which were the anti-submarine patrol bombers, Liberators, Sunderlands, Catalans and Wellingtons. These aircraft eventually dominated the air defences.

By October 1942 16 Liberators had been converted for the anti-submarine role, and in the same month a number were stationed in Iceland. Additional squadrons of the 93rd Bombardment from Nos. 330 and 409 Bomber Squadrons were also operating out of St Eval in Cornwall, England. Other squadrons were stationed in Belfast in Northern Ireland and equipped with modified Liberator Mk.Vs with an additional 200 gallons of fuel and eight x 250 lbs. depth charges. A number were, in May 1943, also equipped with the American Mark 24 acoustic torpedo.

At the beginning of 1943 the German submarine force was at its strongest with 212 boats ready for operation. In the Atlantic there were 164, in the Mediterranean 24, North Sea 21 and Black Sea 3. A U-boat Pack could number from 10 to 16 and was a potent force when working together to attack a single convoy.

Liberator B.Mk.VI. No. 40 Squadron.

Such was the success the allies had gained against Dönitz's force of U-boats that by the end of 1943 his fleet consisted of just 168 boats as during the year he had lost a total of 237 boats. Allied shipping losses were huge, 3,220,137 tons, a total of 537 ships. But during that same period a total of 13 million tons of shipping had been built, the majority being the Liberty ships. The allies were winning the U-boat war and such was their confidence that they began shipping American troops across the ocean to take part in Operation Bolero – the build-up of troops ready for the invasion.

The first of the escort carriers had been switched from the Torch operation in North Africa and new radar techniques were being used on

Liberator B.Mk.VI of No. 5 OTU, British Colombia, 1944/45.

the long range B-24s. This was in the form of very short-range radar equipment which could reflect from small objects at sea and against which the German radar search receiver fitted to the boats was useless. The same British radar was soon to be installed on every battleship in the navy and on a large number of merchantmen.

The first time the U-boat pack came up against the new defence techniques was in May when an outward-bound convoy was delayed by storms and some ships scattered. A pack of twelve submarines had concentrated around the convoy as it regrouped. Two allied support groups sailed from Newfoundland and reached the convoy but not before five ships had been sunk. Eleven U-boats were sunk, and it was a salutary lesson for Dönitz as he lost more and more of his boats to the support groups. Five U-boats were also lost when attacking a fast convoy, which suffered no losses – it was, at last, the 'turning of the tide'.

In desperation Dönitz ordered his U-boat captains to surface when they sighted convoys and fight it out with the support groups. It was a terrible mistake as the support groups, with their frigates, escort carriers and long-range Liberators, took their toll of the enemy. For three months after that battle there was not a single U-boat in the Atlantic as Dönitz had withdrawn them.

The majority of the American troops were transported by the fast, ocean-going liners such as the Queen Mary and Queen Elizabeth. A total of 680,000 had landed in England and Northern Ireland, and of those 127,000 had then been re-shipped to Africa, Sicily and Italy. The materials such as armaments, food and other war supplies followed them in the Liberty ships.

The claim was made that a single long-range Liberator operating out of Iceland and escorting a convoy could save at least six merchant ships in thirty sorties. The same aircraft used as a bomber against the U-boat pens in France, over a similar period of time, dropped less than 100 tons of bombs with little effect. This information was used to try and persuade 'Bomber' Harris, the C-in-C Bomber Command, and General Spaatz, C-in-C of the 8th Air Force in England, of the benefits of releasing more long-range Liberators for Coastal Command.

Liberator B.Mk.VI of No. 356 Squadron, RASF, SEAC.

Armament of the ASV Liberator was increased by the installation of additional waist guns and by the end of the year they were also armed with rockets, sonar buoys and ninety anti-tank bombs that had been modified for use against the U-boats. Initially, the rate of loss in the Atlantic showed little change from the figures of 1942, and the rate was so high that America declared its intention of withdrawing from the Atlantic. This would have seriously jeopardised the British Atlantic convoys and effectively prevent any build up of American forces for the invasion of the Continent.

Two convoys sailed from Halifax, Nova Scotia, for England, with the first being sighted by a U-boat that radioed the information to the rest of the 'Pack' whereupon they converged on the ships. Over a period of three days the U-boats sank 12 ships. The two convoys merged for mutual protection but a total of 21 ships had been sunk by the time the amalgamated convoy came under the umbrella of anti-submarine aircraft and warships. This was the climax of the Battle of the Atlantic.

President Roosevelt now ordered that large numbers of Liberators would be made available to Coastal Command and, by the end of March, the force had grown to 41. They were fitted with very short-range radar sets which could reflect much smaller objects against which the German search radar, as fitted to the U-boat, was useless. More contacts were made with the submarines and by May considerable progress had been made in the provision of continuous air cover from one side of the Atlantic to the other.

The first major success by all sections of the convoy defence system was when ten U-boats were sunk against a loss of nine ships. A convoy that followed lost three ships but three U-boats were also sunk. Within months the Atlantic situation had changed to the extent that in a convoy shortly after the event mentioned above no ships were lost but five U-boats were sunk. Between April and June the same year 119 U-boats were sunk for relatively small Allied losses – the 'Happy Time' was coming to an end.

Privateer, Patuxent, with totally glazed nose section.

N6815D Navy Privateer. Note nose glazing.

Ex-naval PB4Y-2 with different engines and nose section. N31916

CHAPTER SEVEN

Other Theatres of Operation

It is not well known that a number of Liberators operated at night and were camouflaged Matt Black (Night) for use against German Ground Control Centres. The Liberators carried electronic jamming gear and were capable of carrying out missions lasting several hours. With aid from the RAF, Liberator B-24Hs were equipped and operated by the 36th Bombardment Squadron. They were also used for daylight jamming operations.

No. 223 Squadron, RAF, also used the converted Liberators and from August 23, 1944, flew missions equipped with 'Jostle' jamming devices in their ex-USAAF aircraft. No. 214 Squadron RAF used the Liberator for patrols off the Dutch coastline.

Towards the end of the war five RAF Liberators were operating against the Japanese in the Pacific during daylight hours. A special flight of Liberators was formed to monitor enemy W/T and R/T transmissions in order to plot enemy bombers as they approached a target. Special ELINT (electronic intelligence) was first used by No.159 Squadron, which was formed in January 1942 to operate the ELINT Liberators. In November 1942 the Squadron transferred to the Far East to commence operations against the Japanese in Burma. The Far East was to be its 'home' base until the end of the war with Japan. One of its operations, using 15 Liberators in a round trip of some 3,000 miles, was to mine the approaches to Penang Harbour on the night of October 27/28th, 1944. This operation was repeated in January 1945 with 16 aircraft. One of the last operations of this Liberator squadron, on June 15, 1945, was to bomb and destroy a 10,000 ton Japanese tanker in the Bay of Siam.

Mediterranean Liberators

The largest number of squadrons operating Liberators with the RAF and USAAF were in the Mediterranean Theatre (MTO), the first being No. 108 Squadron, RAF, based in Egypt, which received unarmed Liberators.

B-24H, 491st Bombardment Group. 295123, August 1955.

In January 1943 No. 178 Squadron, RAF, was formed at Shandur, Egypt and was equipped with the Liberator Mk.II (between January 1943 to August 1943) and The Liberator Mk.III (between September 1943 to December 1944). Finally, in January 1944 the Squadron received the Liberator B.VI. From its base in Egypt the Squadron was soon bombing targets in Libya, including Tripoli, but in February 1944 No. 178 Squadron

B-24J, No.52 Squadron, RAF, Foggia. Olive Drab and Grey colour scheme.

moved to Italy to take part in special operations, joining with No.205 Group bombers for raids against targets in northern Italy.

The Group bombed Italy and south-east Europe in conjunction with Bomber Command units based in England. The railway systems in Hungary and Romania were systematically attacked throughout 1943/44. This helped prevent the movement of German troops intended to bolster defences against the Allied landings in Normandy, which the Germans were aware would be made in the summer of 1944.

The waterways of Germany, which carried a vast amount of war and other materials could not be surface damaged, but attacks were launched along the Danube against river traffic by No. 206 Squadron which carried out 'Gardening' (mine dropping) operations. By May 1944 more than 500 miles had been laid with mines by 16 Liberators and 53 Wellingtons. Sorties were flown by night, in particular when there was a full moon, and at very low-level.

The results were excellent and water traffic came to a standstill. Canals were choked with barges unable to move, and by August 1944 the amount of water traffic had dropped by 70 percent.

Pacific Operations
The United States 5th Air Force, in the south-west area of the Pacific, was assigned a total of four Groups, the 22nd, 43rd, 9th and 380th. The 22nd

B-24J, of No.40 Squadron, RAF Foggia, Italy, 1945

traded its twin-engine Mitchells and B-20 Marauder bombers for Liberators in February 1944, and operated them until the end of the war. The 43rd had switched from the Fortress to the Liberator over an extended period from May to September 1943. The other two Groups, the 390th and 380th were equipped with the Liberator at the outset.

The 22nd concentrated mainly on bombing making only a few reconnaissance missions over Japan late in the war. Targets were airfields, shipping and oil fields in Ceran, Halmahera and Borneo. The southern Philippines began receiving attention during September 1944 as the 22nd struck at key targets to pave the way for the Leyte landings and then switched to Luzon. Later, Liberators flew close support for the Australian Army in Borneo and also raided targets in Formosa and China.

The 43rd Group, after receiving its quota of Liberators while stationed in Port Moresby, experimented with skip bombing techniques and employed these tactics against Japanese shipping during the battle for the Bismarck Sea. This mission earned the Group a DUC (Distinguished Unit

B-24J, 308th Bombardment Group, 14th Air Force.

Commendation). The 43rd continued to operate against enemy shipping in the Bismarck Archipelago and off the Dutch East Indies. They also took out airfields and Japanese bases in New Guinea, Yap, the Celebes, Halmahera and the southern Philippines, plus undertaking a number of ultra long-range missions against Ceran and Borneo.

B-24J of the 308th Bombardment Group, 14th Air Force. Note colour scheme of Black undersides.

The Group moved initially to the Philippines and then to Shima and from here they raided airfields, railroad yards and shipping in the Inland Sea and Sea of Japan. The 80th was hurriedly moved to Hawaii in September 1941 and assigned to the 7th Air Force while it completed its training. In November 1942 they moved on to Australia to join the 5th Air Force and were sent into action immediately. For the most part 90th Group's missions were similar to those of the 22nd. They even participated in a number of the same battles. Their DUC was won for raids on Wewak in September 1943 when their Liberators flew through

B-24J, 11th Bombardment Group, 28th Bomb Squadron on route to Truk, Carolina Islands, July 29, 1944.

heavy anti-aircraft fire and fought off fighter patrols.

The 380th, although a member of the 5th Air Force, was attached to the RAAF (Royal Australian Air Force) until January 1945 and shared regular duties and training periods with RAAF combat crews. The Group finally took part in combat in May 1943 and was awarded a DUC for a series of long range attacks on Balikpapan, Borneo, in August 1945. The Group was later awarded a second medal while carrying out support duties on Hollandia. The 380th flew the same type of missions as the other Groups and Squadrons with one exception, when, after the war it was used for ferrying prisoners of war from Japan to Manila.

In the Central Pacific area the 7th Air Force had four Liberator groups, including the 11th, 30th, 307th and 494th. The 11th started its career with the 7th Air Force, was re-assigned and returned once again to the 7th in March 1943. After rejoining this Force the Group was equipped with, and trained to operate, Liberators returning to combat missions the following November.

Operating out of Funafuri they took part in the Marshall, Gilberts and Mariana campaigns before moving on to Guam in October 1944. From their base they attacked the Volcan and Bonib Islands, concentrating upon airfields, shipping and other military installations. The 11th was on Okinawa when the war ended and continued to fly armed reconnaissance missions over China and Manchuria where the Red Army was on the

B-24J, 11th Bomb Group, 432 Bomb Squadron over Kwajalein, Marshall Islands, June 1944

move. The aircraft also ferried PoWs from Okinawa to Japan.

The 30th went into combat from the Ellis Islands during November 1943 and supported the troops invading the Gilbert Islands with the Marines. They moved on to Tarawa and the Marshall Islands, striking at enemy airfields in the area. Moving across to Kwsajelein in March 1944 the B-24s struck Truk, neutralising the area while the main attack on the

Formating B-24J Liberator of 458th Bomb Group, US 8th Air Force.

B-24D Liberator (41-23711) of the 93rd Bomb Group, US 8th AF.

1

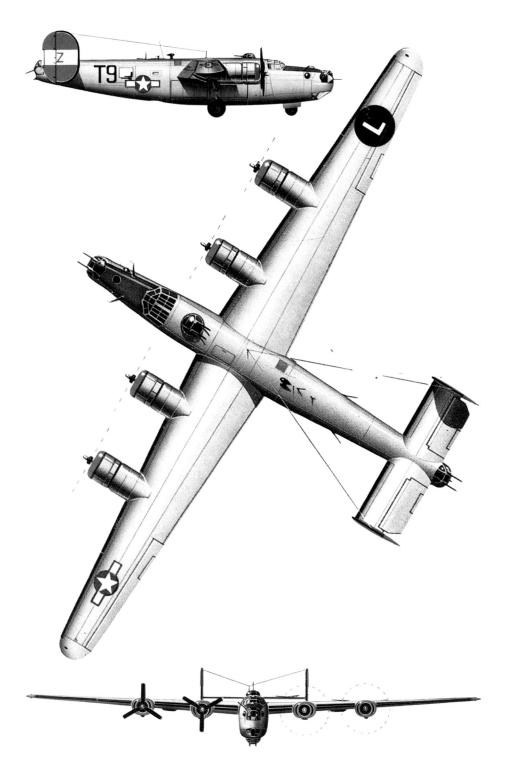

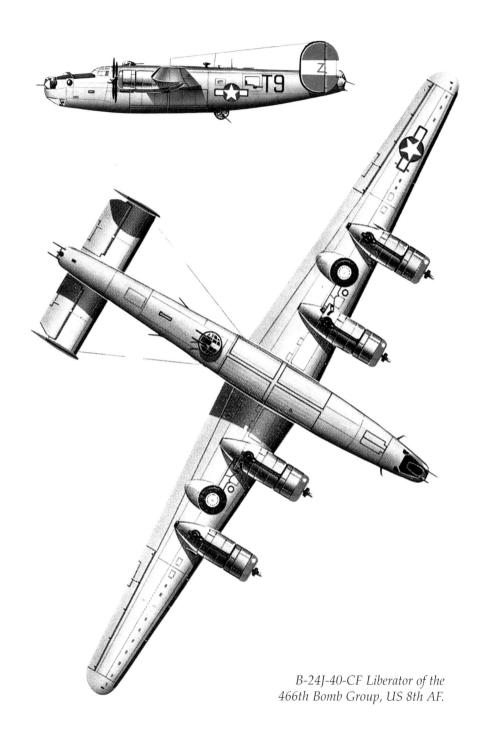

B-24J-40-CF Liberator of the
466th Bomb Group, US 8th AF.

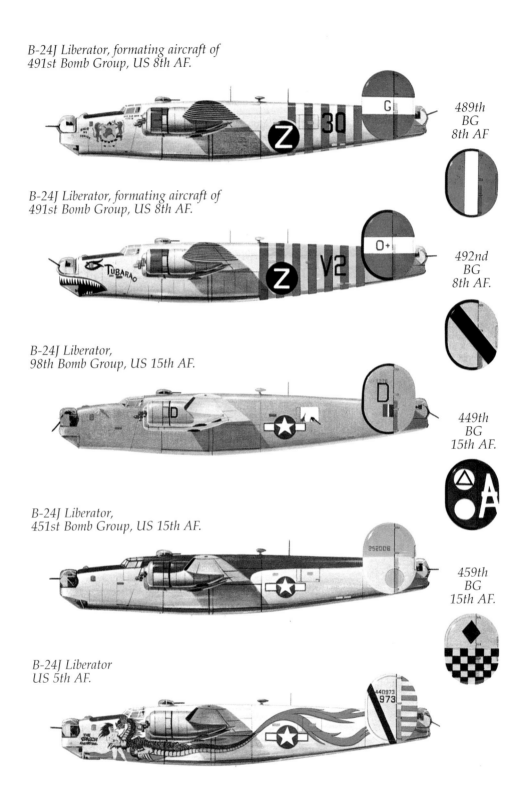

B-24J Liberator, formating aircraft of
491st Bomb Group, US 8th AF.

B-24J Liberator, formating aircraft of
491st Bomb Group, US 8th AF.

B-24J Liberator,
98th Bomb Group, US 15th AF.

B-24J Liberator,
451st Bomb Group, US 15th AF.

B-24J Liberator
US 5th AF.

489th
BG
8th AF

492nd
BG
8th AF.

449th
BG
15th AF.

459th
BG
15th AF.

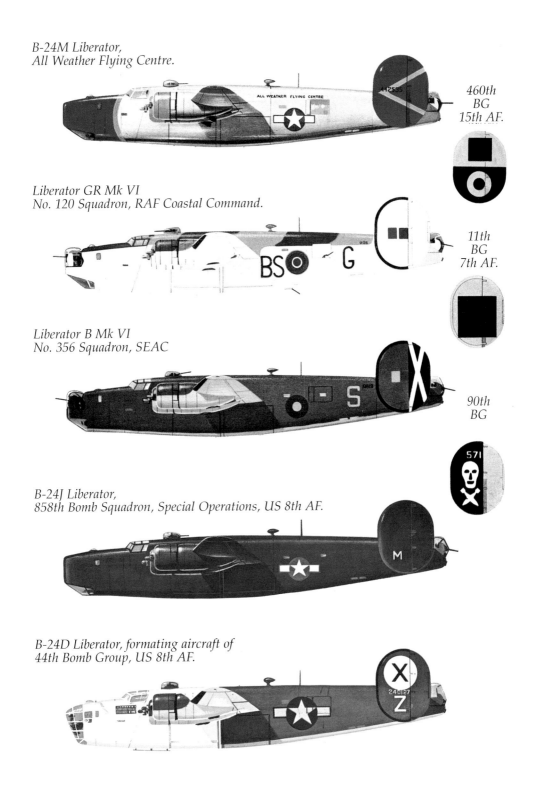

B-24M Liberator,
All Weather Flying Centre.

460th
BG
15th AF.

Liberator GR Mk VI
No. 120 Squadron, RAF Coastal Command.

11th
BG
7th AF.

Liberator B Mk VI
No. 356 Squadron, SEAC

90th
BG

B-24J Liberator,
858th Bomb Squadron, Special Operations, US 8th AF.

B-24D Liberator, formating aircraft of
44th Bomb Group, US 8th AF.

B-24D Liberator
93rd Bomb Group, US 8th AF.

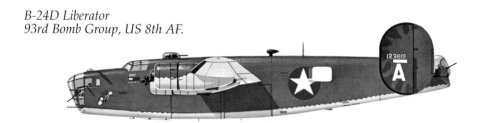

B-24D Liberator 'Hellsadroppin'
93rd Bomb Group, US 8th AF.

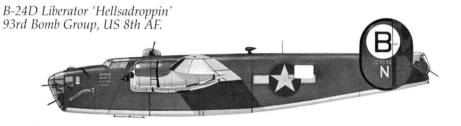

B-24J Liberator 'The Sky Shark'
389th Bomb Group, US 8th AF.

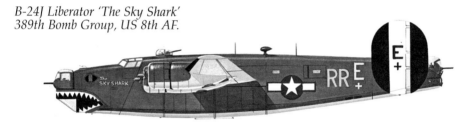

Liberator C.VIII
No. 53 Squadron, R AF.

Liberator B.VIII
No. 86 Squadron, R AF.

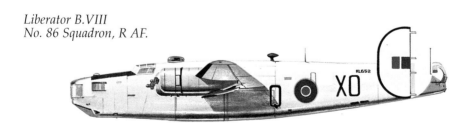

Liberator GR.III
No. 120 Squadron, RAF Coastal Command.

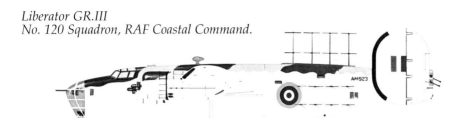

Liberator GR.VI
No. 311 Squadron (Czechoslovakian), RAF Coastal Command.

B-24J Liberator
No. 201 Flight, Royal Australian Air Force.

Liberator GR.VI
No. 321 Squadron, Koninklijke Marine, Dutch East Indies.

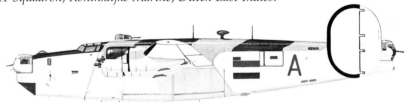

Liberator GR.VI
No. 311 Squadron (Czechoslovakian), RAF Coastal Command.

B-24M Liberator
Chinese National Air Force

B-24J Liberator
No. 24 Squadron, Royal Australian Air Force.

B-24J Liberator
Indian Air Force.

LB-30Liberator
One of 15 repossessed by US from a British (ex French) contract.

B-24J Liberator
90th Bomb Group, US 5th AF. (SW Pacific)

B-24L Liberator 'Bolivar Jr'
431st Bomb Squadron, 11th Bomb Group, US 7th AF.

B-24J Liberator.
11th Bomb Group, US 7th AF.

B-24L Liberator
US 7th AF (unit unknown),

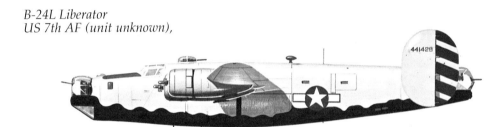

B-24J Liberator
375th Bomb Squadron, 308th Bomb Group, US 14th AF.

B-24M Liberator

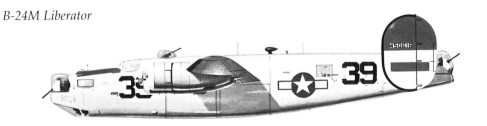

B-24M Liberator 'Billie K'
461st Bomb Group, US 15th AF (Italy)

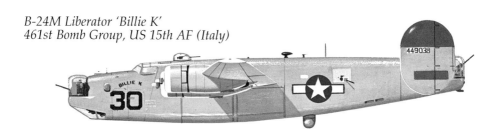

B-24J Liberator 'Minnesota Mauler'
451st Bomb Group, US 15th AF (Italy)

B-24J Liberator
449th Bomb Group, US 15th AF (Italy)

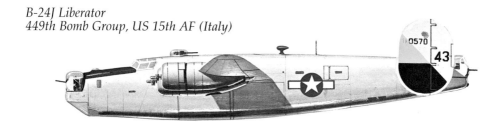

B-24J Liberator '
460th Bomb Group, US 15th AF (Italy)

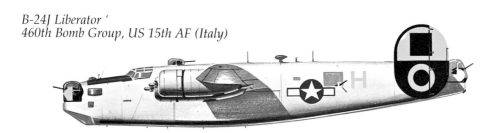

B-24J Liberator '
465th Bomb Group, US 15th AF (Italy)

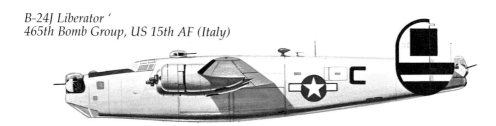

B-24D Liberator 'Strawberry Bitch'
512th Bomb Squadron, 376th Bomb Group, US 9th AF (Desert).

B-24D Liberator
28th Bomb Group, US 11th AF (Aleutians).

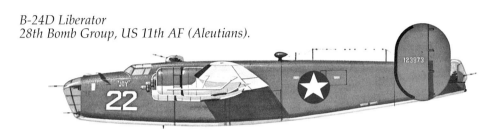

B-24D Liberator
In Sea-searcg camouflage.

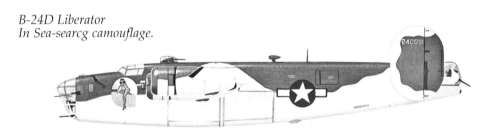

C-109 Liberator
XIth Troop Carrier Command (Europe)

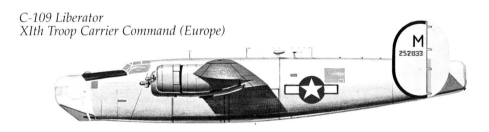

EZB-24 Liberator
Aero Icing Research Laboratory.

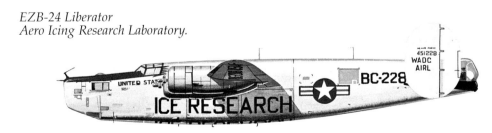

Liberator B.VI
No. 356 Squadron, RAF, (SEAC)

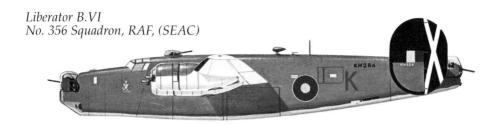

Liberator B.VI

Liberator B.VII
No, 355 Squadron, RAF, (SEAC)

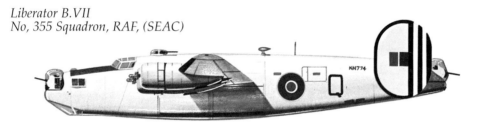

Liberator B.VI
No. 104 Squadron, RAF, (SEAC)

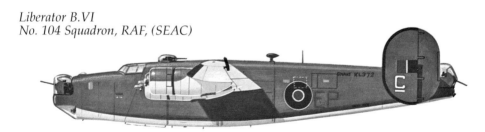

Liberator B.VI

'Formating' B-24 Liberators

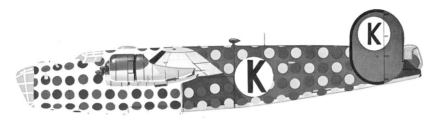

B-24D Liberator, 458th Bomb Group, US 8th AF.

B-24J Liberator, 458th Bomb Group,US 8th AF.

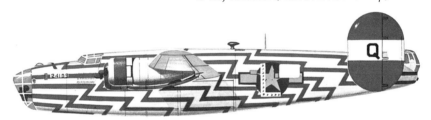

B-24D Liberator, 466th Bomb Group, US 8th AF.

B-24D Liberator, 445th Bomb Group, US 8th AF.

B-24D Liberator
44th Bomb Group, US 8th AF.

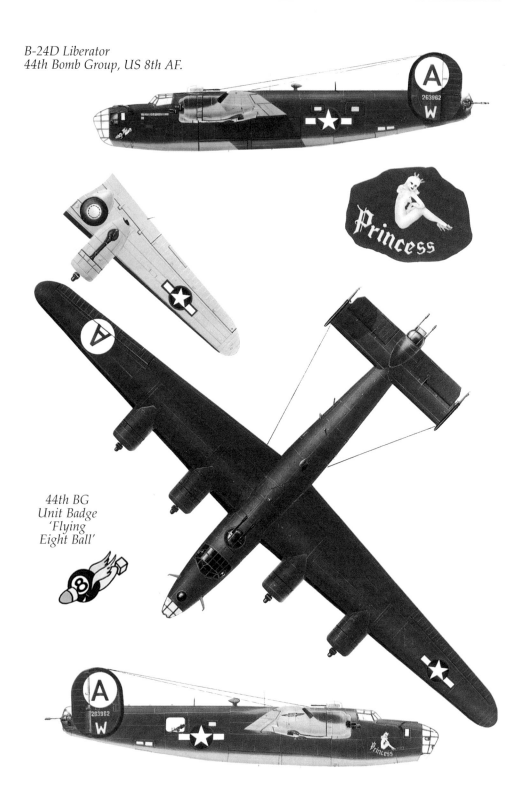

44th BG
Unit Badge
'Flying
Eight Ball'

*B-24D Liberator
67th Bomb Squadron,
44th Bomb Group, US 8th AF.*

*B-24D Liberator,
93rd Bomb Group, US 8th AF.*

*B-24D-5-CO Liberator
USAAF Anti-Submarine.*

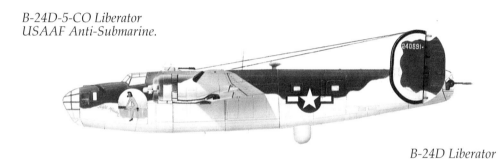

*B-24D Liberator
376th Bomb Group, US 9th AF.
Command Aircraft on the
Ploesti Oil Refineries, August 1,*

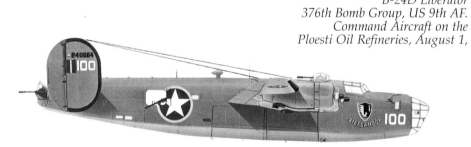

*B-24D Liberator
90 th Bomb Group, US 5th AF.
SW Pacific.*

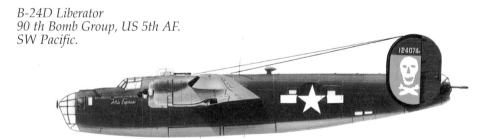

B-24J Liberator, 'Alley Oop', of the 780th Bomb Squadron, 465th Bomb Group, US 15th AF.

B-24D Liberators at the bomber crew Training School, Hammer Field, California.

Marianas was launched. They also struck at Guam, Saipan, and the Wake Islands in 1944 to get established on Saipan which had fallen to the Allies. From their new base the bombers attacked the Bonin and Volcan Islands in support of the American forces invading Iwo Jima, and continued to strike at the bypassed areas in the Carolinas and Marianas until finally ordered back to Hawaii to test and re-equip in 1945.

During the battle for Iwo Jima the 7th Air Force pounded the island continuously over a period of 19 days before the Marines considered it possible to land on February 19, 1945. The bloody battles lasted for four weeks, instead of the estimated three to four days, such was the fighting ability of the Japanese ground forces.

The 307th started operations by flying search and patrol missions from Hawaii but, from December 1942 until January the following year, using the Midway Islands as a base, they bombed Wake Island. Later they moved to Guadalcanal, when it had been secured, to become part of the 13th Air Force.

The 494th moved to Palua in September 1944 but, before it could be in a position to start operations, personnel had to aid in the construction of their new bases. When the Auguar base was completed the bombers were launched against Yap and Korar Islands and also struck at other bypassed areas. Later the Philippines came in for a major share of operations with

Group of B-24Js attacking Japanese positions on Iwo Jima.

bombers hitting various targets on Corregidor and Caballo moving up the main islands, with the Japanese on Clark Field becoming the prime target. In early 1943 they started flying strike missions against Mindanao air bases and supply depots in the Davao Gulf and Iullana Bay areas.

Moving on to Okinawa the next operation was to launch a bombing campaign against airfields in Kyushu and this continued until the war ended with VJ Day. The Group had, prior to that date, dropped propaganda leaflets and incendiary bombs on various Japanese cities. Finally, when the war was over, they transported personnel and materials from Manilla to Tokyo.

The South-West Pacific area was the stamping ground of the 13th Air Force and its two Groups, the 5th and 307th. The first was an old

B-24J, 43rd Bomb Group, 5th Air Force, New Guinea.

established Group that dated back to August 1919 when it was formed in Hawaii – the Group's motto was 'Kaai Oka Lews', or 'The Guardian of the Upper Region'. Leaving the island of Hawaii in November 1942 they joined the 13th Air Force at Espiritu Sano, arriving there on December 1. Many long-range photo-reconnaissance missions were scheduled for the

Group in the Solomons and over the Coral Sea, along with attacks against Bougainville, New Britain, New Ireland and Woleai, where the Group won its first DUC for action over the bitterly defended Wolaei Island.

New targets were assigned against Yap, Truk and Palaus which were bombed to pave the way for the Leyte operation. A second DUC was awarded to the Group for a raid on the Balikpapan oil refineries on September 30, 1944. The unit went on to fly numerous missions in the Philippines until the end of the war

The 30th Group joined the 13th Air Force on Guadalcanal and operated in the area with the 5th Air Force. They won the DUC for an unescorted daylight attack on Truk on March 29, 1944, and their second award was for an attack on Balikpapan which had proved to be one of the strongest targets in the area. Finally, they operated with the 5th Air Force which, at that time, was providing support for the Australian troops fighting in Borneo. They also bombed targets in Indo-China during the final three months of the war. After the war had ended they ferried PoWs from Okinawa to Manilla.

The 6th Air Force in the Panama Zone had two groups of B-24s assigned and based in the area, the 6th and 9th, both being senior Groups. The 6th dated from 1919 and the 9th from 1922 when they were formed

B-24D of the 7th Bombardment Group, 10th Air Force, India.

in the Canal Zone. Both flew anti-submarine patrols and when the 6th disbanded on November 1, 1943, both it, and the 9th, returned to the United States. They were used as training cadres for various bomb groups and to test new equipment with mixed complements of B-24s, B-17s and B-26s.

In the Canal Zone of the Interior three of the four numbered Air Forces, the 1st, 2nd and 4th had B-24 Groups attached. The first had the 400th and 471st and the 4th had the 399th and 470th Groups. There was a large Liberator Air Force in America, the 2nd with eight Groups attached; the 302nd, 332nd, 346th, 383rd, 400th, 470th and 471st. All of these Groups were engaged in training operations with their main duties consisting of training complete combat crews or individual replacements for overseas Groups to fill gaps when crew had lost members in combat.

The Liberators found their way, in small batches, to various other training schools later in the war. Thus a fledging gunner or cadet

B-24D, 272956, of the 90th Bombardment Group 'Jolly Rogers'. Called 'Betsy'. On way to targets in New Guinea, 22 February 1944.

bombardier might find themselves firing from a gun-turret or dropping bombs from the same type of aircraft before they could be assigned to a combat squadron.

On June 29 yet another battle between the opposing forces in the Pacific occured when the Americans landed on the Solomon Islands and they were attacked in the Kula Gulf by the Japanese who were reinforcing New Georgia. Six Japanese destroyers were sunk by a combination of aircraft and American warships. On August 6 Japanese warships, packed with troops on their way to reinforce the main Japanese forces at

Kolombangra, were intercepted. Throughout all these actions the Liberator was to prove its worth with its long-range capability and method of attack.

B-24J, 494th Bombardment Group, 864th Bomb Squadron, Yontan, on way to bomb Japan.

The concerted Allied offensive started in Burma in the Spring of 1943 when the British 14th Army advanced, in appalling weather, with the support of Wellingtons and Liberators. No. 355 Squadron, RAF, had recently been formed in the area and flew its Liberators to South East Asia where they were soon to be attacking targets in Mandalay. The British and American forces in the area were combined to form SEAC (South East Asia Command), and the Japanese advance into Impala in March 1944 was soon driven back.

The 10th US Air Force operated from landing strips hacked out of the jungle which tended to bog down the Liberators with its large undercarriage wheels. The 10th attacked Japanese shipping and took part in the operations *Earthquake* and *Major*. Long-range operations restricted the bomb loads that the Liberators could carry, but experiments with fuel soon enabled an increase in bomb loads and fuel requirements. Bomb loads were raised to 8,000 lbs. once again.

The Strategic Air Force flew hundreds of missions using the Liberator, which was becoming the work-horse of the Pacific, with more and more additional squadrons being formed. No. 354 Squadron, RAF, operated

Liberator C-109 Tanker conversion of B-24J. Burma.

out of Ceylon with Liberators on anti-submarine patrols, while other units sowed mines in the Rangoon area.

In 1945 veteran RAF squadrons from Europe began joining the Liberator force as part of the Heavy Conversion Units in India. When the war was over they switched to dropping of food supplies to Allied prisoners of war. In Europe, during the final days, old war weary Liberators were utilised for Operation *Anvil*. This was the conversion of bombers into drones with the fitting of a large warhead in the nose section in an attempt to destroy the V2 rocket sites that were aimed at London. Numbers of Liberators were designated as PB4Ys, when operated by the US Navy as the Privateer, long-range, armed, reconnaissance squadrons.

Initially the USAAF operated B-24Ds on anti-submarine patrols, a duty the US Navy felt rightfully belonged to them. On July 7, 1945, an agreement was reached whereby the USN would be allotted a number of aircraft and as soon as they were ready to relieve the Air Force they

PBY-2 Privateer, US Navy.

would take command of all ocean and anti-submarine duties.

The Liberator was the chosen aeroplane which the Navy designated as the PB4Y, and by the end of the war had received a total of 977. By August 1943 the Navy began replacement of the twin-fin modified Liberators for the new design PB4Y-1 Privateers. On May 3, 1943, CVAC had been authorised to withdraw three B-24Ds from the Consolidated production line to convert them into PB4Y-1 experimental prototypes. In time the Navy had 739 examples of this new type. The PB4Y-2 was officially given the name Privateer, the name already used by Navy personnel, and it was in service before the end of the war. A large number continued operations after the war and a transport plane, the RY-3, was also produced.

PBY-2 Privateer, US Navy.

The 403rd had the dubious honour of becoming the last unit to be operating on June 6, 1944. The 494th was part of the 7th Air Force in the Pacific equipped with the Model B-24J Liberator, and it started operations

PB4Y-1 Chinese Nationalist Air Force.

against the Japanese in the winter of that year. Liberators of the USAAF reached their maximum strength with a grand total of 6,000 plus B-24s spread over 177 squadrons, in addition there were six special squadrons operating overseas. Forty Bomb Groups of 184 squadrons were eventually established.

Liberators in Allied Air Forces

A number of Allied nations also flew the type during and after the war. The Royal Air Force made extensive use of the Liberator obtaining over 2,000 of these aircraft from the Mk.I through to the GR Mk.VII anti-submarine type. The Royal Air Force operated 41 squadrons equipped with the B-24, and a number of others had Liberators as part of their equipment, normally the heavy bomber squadrons. In the Mediterranean, Nos. 37, 40, 70, 104, 148, 178 and 614 squadrons flew the B-24. While in the Far East the Liberator served with the following numbered squadrons, 99, 159, 160, 203, 215, 232, 233, 234, 246, 321, 355, 356, 357 and 358. In the United Kingdom several squadrons were equipped with the Liberator including Nos. 53, 59, 86, 102, 203, 224, 233, 292, 301, 411, 423, 426, 505 and 547.

Also, for a short period, Nos. 53 and 59 squadrons operated from Iceland with Nos. 206 and 220, flying from the Azores on convoy protection and anti-submarine duties. In the Far East the RAAF was

B-24J of the Indian Air Force.

represented by Nos. 21, 23, 24, and 25 squadrons, using them mainly for night bombing missions.

Transport versions made an early appearance in British colours carrying the letter 'C' in front of the mark number. One was fitted out as a personal aircraft for Winston Churchill and named 'Commando'.

The Liberator served the RAF long and well, and many were still in service when the Berlin Airlift was undertaken in 1948. Commonwealth countries such as Australia, South Africa and New Zealand, all received numbers of Liberators, and in the immediate post-war period a large number found their way into the service of many Latin American air forces.

Even today a few continue service as freighters. Indeed in Bolivia, they were operated as transports for many years. The British Aircraft

A number of Liberators were used by BOAC as transports during the war. This one is at Prestwick.

Corporation (BOAC) still had a few in service after the war, and the Confederate Air Force of America still has one in flying condition.

The USAAF Air Museum has one on display and there is a second in the National Air Museum's collection. Recently a group of enthusiasts in

San Diego have been attempting to collect sufficient money to ferry one back to America. In Britain a B-24L example of this venerable war-horse can be seen at the Aerospace Museum at Cosford in Shropshire. A few were converted to water carrying fire bombers and may still exist in the Pacific, North West and Canada, but the vast majority went the way of all old military aircraft, to the smelter's furnaces.

CHAPTER EIGHT

The Choice of Battlefield

When a cross Channel invasion of the northern European coast was ruled out for 1943, the question arose of what to do with the forces already available. The United States strongly argued that a larger share of Allied resources should be used in the Pacific war. Churchill was anxious to strike at the 'Soft Under Belly' of the Axis forces in the Mediterranean area and this, coupled with the intensive bombing of Germany, would keep them engaged until the main invasion started.

Both General Marshall, Chief of Staff of the American Army, and Admiral King, the Chief of Staff of Naval Operation, also believed that Germany had to be defeated first before the main attacks were directed at the Japanese. But, they also felt that operations against Southern France were not necessary.

Admiral King had estimated that the percentage of total war effort of all the Allies, including Russia and China, employed in the Pacific amounted to just 15 percent, with Europe, the Atlantic and the D-Day build-up, consuming a huge 85 percent.

King and Marshall considered that this imbalance could be fatal. Although Germany was the number one target, they stated that unless the initiative was continued against Japan the situation could arise where Allied forces would have to be diverted to the Pacific to contain Japan if the Allies were to shorten the war. At least 30 percent of all total war effort should be transferred immediately.

The Australian Contribution
The most obvious countries from which to build-up the Pacific offensive, outside America, were in the Antipodes, Australia and New Zealand.

B-24M of the Chinese Nationalist Air Force.

English was the major language and there was room for the great build-up for the offensive against Japan without the need to cut down jungles and build rough landing strips. There were 'safe' harbours and room for training of ground, air and naval forces.

In 1943 the Allied Air Force, South West Pacific Area, was commanded by Lieut. General Kenney and by April of that year a review revealed that the United States had nine fighter squadrons, five dive bomber, six medium and general reconnaissance bomber, eight heavy bomber and eight transport aircraft, a total of 36 squadrons.

Australia could only contribute 31 squadrons of which none were heavy bombers and only nine were fighters. Only one Liberator squadron existed, No. 329. The specific tasks allotted to the Royal Australian Air Force (RAAF) was the offensive against enemy forward bases established on Timor, New Britain, New Guinea and the Solomon Islands.

The US 5th Air Force in Australia and New Guinea had received a total of 2,284 aircraft and out of those only 772 were available for immediate action. The 5th Air Force was responsible for operations in Papua, New Guinea and north-east Australia, in addition to the overall responsibility of reconnaissance and bomber operations, but it lacked sufficient heavy bombers.

B-24J of No. 12 Squadron RAAF at a repair depot.

Of the 60 Liberator squadrons available in No. 90 Group only 15 were available for operations. In New Guinea there were nine American and two Australian fighter squadrons. The majority of the Japanese squadrons opposing the Australian forces were based at Rabaul and the northern Solomons. However, there was one thing crucially in favour of the Allies, the over-extension of Japanese naval power. Losses in ships

B-24J, No 7 OTU, Tocumkual, RAAF.

and aircraft could not be easily replaced due to a shortage of materials and skilled labour at home and the inability to rush reinforcements to the vast Pacific area over which the Japanese forces were spread.

The advantage held by the Allies was that they could strike where they pleased. Japanese strongholds were in existence but they could be attacked as and when the Allies had built up their forces. In the meantime all efforts were made to deprive Japanese from obtaining reinforcements. The Japanese high command had decided that these reinforcements from Japan had to get to their destination, but due to the pressure exerted by the American and Australian submarine fleets many vital convoys were sent to the bottom of the Pacific Ocean. For that the Japanese had little answer.

The Allied forces in Australia did have medium bombers such as the Boston and Mitchell and also the Beaufighter and Beaufort torpedo bomber, but their heavy bomber force had to be reinforced. One of the first attacks combining Liberator and Mitchell bombers, escorted by Beaufighters, was in May 1943 when they attacked Lae airfield on Madang.

Three Liberators of No. 319 Squadron, RAAF, bombed Ambon town and, at the end of May, Mitchells, Beaufighters, Liberators and Hudsons attacked enemy airfields in Timor. During May and June reinforcements

Liberator of the RAF with fin flash both inside and outside of fin. Sumatra, Pacific area.

in the shape of Liberator bombers were delivered to the 5th Air Force in the Northern Territory, Australia, and the 381st Bombardment Group with the 528th, 529th, 530th and 531st Squadrons were available for action. Macassar was attacked and during June the Liberators had carried out 50 sorties.

The Japanese replied by attacking the Liberators based at Fenton but Allied radar identified a force of Japanese 'Betty' bombers accompanied by 23 fighters. Spitfires from No. 457 Squadron, with Nos. 542 and 54, were scrambled and attacked the Japanese force which, however, had arrived at its target and destroyed three Liberators. Eight enemy aircraft were claimed for the loss of six Spitfires, three with engine trouble.

As the raids against Fenton continued Allied forces were landing in the Solomon Islands and New Guinea. To divert the enemy's attention from New Guinea, Liberators bombed Kendari, but the Japanese, too, were attacking the Liberator base at Fenton. On July 6 a force of 20 Japanese bombers dropped bombs on the airfield but only destroyed one Liberator.

Mitchells, Hudsons and Liberators attacked Japanese airfields at Penfui, Cape Chater, Bao, Nabire, Fuiloro and Selaru, and the following day Liberators of No. 380 Group attacked Penui airfield. On July 10 a flight of the 531st Squadron raided Babo, then attacked Macassar, in the Celebes, on the 18th. On the 22nd their targets were in Surabaya, Java, damaging refineries and the docks.

Liberators and B-17s attacked Nadzab and Heath's Plantation as a force of American fighters, protecting accompanying transports, watched as the American 504th Parachute regiment were dropped. Bougainville was about to be attacked and as a diversion Americans bombers attacked Rabaul with 49 Liberators striking the Japanese airfield on 23 October. In November, when the Japanese sent reinforcements to Rabaul and Kenney, a force of 27 Liberators and 67 escorting Lightnings were sent to attack the dock area.

The north-western area of Australia was reinforced in August 1943 with the 528th, 529th, 530th and 531st Liberator squadrons and Australian Spitfire, Beaufighter and Lightning fighters. On October 25 four B-24s bombed Pomelaa, in the Celebes, after the greater part of the force had to turn back due to technical faults. Two of the attacking B-24s were shot down.

On December 6, Liberator and Mitchell bombers attacked Borpop airfield in Rabaul. In March 1944 the 5th Air Force started large scale bombing attacks in preparation for the Hollandia operation and in six days dropped 1,600 tons of bombs in attacks on Wewak and other

B-24J 44093 of the 494th Bombardment Group. 'Kuuipo'.

airfields. On the 30th 65 Liberators escorted by Lightnings attacked Hollandia and the attackers included No. 65 Squadron, RAAF.

During April the 5th Air Force attacked targets in New Guinea and also dropped more bombs on Hollandia. Liberators of the 380th Bomber Group struck at targets in Hollandia. In August the RAAF's first Liberator force went into action and made attacks against Japanese shipping near the Banda Islands. Liberators of No. 24 Squadron arrived in Darwin, the first of a planned seven.

No. 24 Squadron attacked an enemy convoy in the Molucca and registered several hits. The squadron joined the 380th Group in September, and on the night of November 27/28th, No. 215 Squadron struck at the docks in Rangoon. In March 1945 Liberators of No. 82 Wing flew many operations against Japanese shipping and sank seven. Six B-24s of No. 24 Squadron, RAAF, joined with others from No. 82 Wing to strike Mapin on the Sumbawa Island.

On April 4 a convoy consisting of a Japanese cruiser and four other ships was spotted in the Flores Sea. RAAF Intelligence concluded they were making for Timor and it was planned to hit the force on the morning of the 6th using B-24s from No. 82 Wing. The actual bombing force consisted of Mitchell bombers and Liberators from Nos. 21 and 24 RAAF squadrons. They attacked from high altitude and were immediately

B-24J, 494th Bombardment Group, 867th Squadron, 7th Air Force.

attacked by Japanese fighters.

In January 1945 the Strategic Air Force mounted a heavy attack against Rangoon when Liberators and B-29s escorted by 67 P-38 Lightnings and P-47 Thunderbolts destroyed Japanese supply dumps. RAAF squadrons Nos. 99, 215 and 355 were part of the B-24 force. In February B-24s of Nos. 99 and 215 squadrons attacked Japanese held targets along the Irrawaddy. B-24s bombed airfields in Borneo, Celebes and Java, and in June Java was attacked in daylight by B-24s of No. 24 Squadron, bombing Maland airfield. On the 15th of the month Australian Liberators bombed positions on Balikpapan and in the same month attacked, again destroying oil installations.

The fighting ended the following month, July, when the atomic bombs had been dropped on the Japanese homeland and the surrender took place on the August 14, 1945. The Liberator's offensive task in the Pacific was over but it had provided the major part of the Allied bomber forces throughout those arduous years.

B-24 at Pottava, Russia, April 11, 1945

B-24 transport conversion for the RCAF, No.168 Squadron. Note engine-cowling shape.

CHAPTER NINE

The B-24's Escort Fighters

As previously mentioned the US 8th Air Force were protected by the escort fighter, normally the USAAF interceptors but at times the Royal Air Force contributed Spitfires for the first stage of the journey, turning back to their bases when the long range P-47 Thunderbolts took over their duties.

It is interesting to compare the Luftwaffe fighter tactics during the Battle of Britain with those of the American long range bombers. The German Messerschmitt bf 109 and the Me 110 fighters were ordered by their Commander, Hermann Göring, to fly close to the bomber forces and attempt to meet the attacking Spitfires and Hurricanes as they swept into the attack. As the Germans aircraft had to keep alongside their charges their fuel drained away and they were often forced to turn back to their French bases with almost dry tanks, leaving the attacking bombers to the mercy of the British fighters.

The evolution of the long-range escort fighter of the USAAF started with the Republic P-47 Thunderbolt. When the first heavy day bombers arrived in England in the summer of 1942 heavy losses were predicted in deep penetrations over the Continent of Europe, ably defended by the Luftwaffe. All this experience was discouraged by comparison with the German fighters during the Battle of Britain.

However, early losses of the B-17E Fortress were not as high as anticipated as they made the 'Milk Runs' over France. But, when in early 1943, the American bombers started attacking German targets losses increased due to formidable enemy opposition. The bomber escorts, the P-47, were nominally short-range fighters and could not fly long distance missions and meet the short-range German fighters on equal terms. The

Allied fighters were in the same position as the Germans were during the Battle of Britain. Something had to be done if the 8th Air Force was to attack the many German targets in France.

A radius of approximately 100 miles was considered to be the maximum to be gained efficiently from a single-seat fighter such as the Spitfire and P-47. Initially the Americans attempted a novel idea of

B-24D of the 28th Bombardment Group, 11th Air Force.

bomber protection by developing the long-range fighter development of the Fortress, the XB-40 as narrated above. The production YB-40 Fortress carried a total of fourteen .50 calibre heavy machine-guns in five twin-gun turrets, a chin turret under the nose, two dorsal, a belly ball turret and additional waist and nose.

However, the weight of this enormous number of guns, turrets and extra ammunition made the YB-40 slow and just as vulnerable as its charges, more so as it could not keep station with the main bomber force to and from the target. Any attempt by YB-40s to accompany bombers slowed the whole formation down normally, with disastrous consequences.

The answer to this problem was immediately obvious, an agile, fast-climbing, hard hitting fighter with a performance equal to, or better than, that of the opposing enemy fighters. This fighter would offer protection against the hordes of defending enemy fighters. Spitfires of the RAF

B-24D, 376th Bombardment Group, 15th Air Force, taxies through floodwater. Italy.

protected the bomber force at the start and end of each mission and the USAAF provided the longer range machines, primarily the P-47 Thunderbolt, but even this had limited range. By this method the bomber formations were protected to some degree and the USAAF had to wait until a true, long-range fighter could be produced.

The RAF already possessed such a fighter, the de Havilland Mosquito, but the British aircraft manufacturer's factories were full of orders. True, the Canadians were also building the Mosquito but only in bomber form as they were urgently required by RAF Bomber Command. At one time the Americans did consider producing the Mosquito themselves, especially as the American Commanders of the 8th Air Force asked for them. The British knew they could not sufficiently increase production and the American government appeared reluctant to produce the Mosquitoes in America.

The immediate answer to the problem was the appearance of the P-47C Thunderbolt which had a 255 gallon internal fuel supply, more than twice that of the Spitfire, and they were able to escort the 8th Air Force bombers further than any other single-seat fighter had done. Strangely the Americans did have a longer-range fighter at the time that could provide an escort for the bombers for the complete journey. It was the Lockheed P-38 Lightning, a twin-engine, twin-boom, heavily armed aircraft. But it had been allocated to the Pacific Theatre where the missions were even longer than the European, although they never had to encounter the agony of the 8th Air Force bombers.

The escort fighter position improved when the Thunderbolts were equipped with shackles for a 200 gallon drop fuel tank, thus increasing the range. The improved P-47D had both wing and fuselage drop tanks in addition to an increased internal tank. The fighter's gross weight increased alarmingly but fortunately the increase in engine power was resolved at the same time. The P-47D was the heaviest single-seat, single-engine fighter in service at that time and it now had a radius of 600 miles, which took it into Germany but still short of the longer journeys such as the attacks on Berlin.

The superb P-51 Mustang, powered by the Rolls-Royce Merlin 61

B-24J, 449th Bombardment Group, with flak damaged rear fuselage. 15th Air Force, Italy.

Series engines, at last resolved the range problem. The USAAF and RAF Mustangs (P-51B and Mk.III) were able to escort the bomber squadrons all the way to the most distant targets in Germany and return to base when it began escort duties in January 1944. It had a longer range, higher speed and ceiling than any other contemporary type. By the beginning of 1945 the Mustang was providing almost all the escorts for the American bombers, although by this time a Spitfire version equipped with long-range fuel tanks could complete the same distances. It was the Rolls-Royce engine that powered both fighters, without which the American long-range bombing missions would have lacked the true escort fighter. At times more than 700 long-range fighters would accompany the bomber missions, but it must be borne in mind that by the summer of 1945 the German Luftwaffe lacked sufficient number of trained pilots and was ground down. Even the P-47 had been improved as the P-47N and could fly with its stable mates. Also, it tended to be used alongside the Hawker Typhoon as a successful Tactical Air Force fighter.

The Lockheed P-38J and L Lightning were used exclusively as escorts for the strategic day bombers of the US 15th Air Force flying from Italy. The P-38L variant had additional internal fuel tanks installed in the wing leading edges plus the normal, large ventral drop tanks.

The Allied Air Forces had triumphed against those of the Axis Powers using the same fighter aircraft developed at the beginning of the war and developed accordingly. This account of the bomber and its escort fighters reveals the enormous efforts and achievements of the Allies. Without such a force the war would have gone on much longer than it did. Air Power had demonstrated the future of military conflict.

B-24J, 455th Bombardment Group, 15th Air Force. 278425.

Convair RY-1 Liberator

CHAPTER TEN

The Liberator Super Bomber – the B-32 Dominator

No story of the Liberator would be complete without the inclusion of the B-32 Dominator, developed as a 'Super' bomber from the basic design of the B-24.

The Consolidated Model 53 XB-32 was one of two LRBs (Long-Range Bombers) that were developed and built to the same specification that eventually produced the Boeing B-29 Super Fortress. The B-32 failed in that it took too long to bring into production and the development of the Boeing B-29 was well advanced when the Consolidated Company submitted their design along with others. It also lacked that vital ingredient, a pressure cabin that the B-29 had.

Like the majority of the established aircraft manufacturers Consolidated (now Convair) had a long history of designing and building large aircraft for both the civil and military markets, and was also capable of developing a Super Bomber for the USAAF.

To put both the B-24 and B-32 into context and to show the continuation of the basic design we examine the total background of the XBLR (Experimental Bomber, Long-Range) that started in the early 1930s

Final development of the LRBs
The B-17 had entered service in 1938 and the US Army Air Corps required that Boeing design an updated model suitable for high altitude operations with the aid of a pressurized cabin. This was first presented as the Model 2991. A second proposal, in March of that year, along the same lines was the Boeing Model 316, this being a large aeroplane, almost an improved XB-15 to be powered by four Wright Cyclone 2,000-hp R-3350 radial engines. The design was accepted by the Air Force as the XB-20,

which featured a pressurized cabin and was different to any other previous Boeing designs having a wing with a small, parallel, centre section with equi-tapered outer panels.

The fuselage, a streamlined oval structure, had a wing mounted in the shoulder (high) position, and the fin and rudder of graceful design blended into the rear fuselage. The Air Force also wanted a bomber of greater range than that of the Fortress and declared that such an aeroplane would have to carry a 4,000 lb. bomb load over a distance of 4,000 miles while possessing high altitude performance. Not long after these proposals were made the USAAC had a change of heart and cancelled the two ordered prototypes, although the Model 316D (Y1B-20) was to remain a project.

B-24J, 308th Bombardment Group, 14th Air Force. 375th Squadron.

Later in March 1938, Boeing was to produce another design for a long-range bomber, based loosely upon the Model 316 with a pressure cabin, using standard B-17 wings, engines and tail unit married to a large diameter fuselage and tri-cycle undercarriage. Bearing the Boeing Model number 322 it, too, was abandoned by the Boeing design team who decided it was impracticable to build.

What was more to the point was the reluctance of the Air Force to make

B-24J, 43rd Bombardment Group, 5th Air Force. Note fin/rudder markings.

funding available for the new project as it was committed to a long production run of the Fortress. The Model 322 would have been powered by four of the new Pratt & Whitney R-2180 engines of 1,400-hp as specified for the Model 316. One of the major problems facing the Boeing engineers was pressurizing the gun positions and this led to a reduction in the number of defensive guns fitted to four – too few to provide for a good defence against enemy day fighters, which were also improving.

With the demise of their Model 322, Boeing offered the Air Force a Private Venture design which would encompass all the experience gained with the range of designs and construction of large bombers. The Model 333 also appeared in 1938 such was the rate of progress, but there was no official funding and the company had to accept the entire financial risk.

The new design included two pressurized crew compartments connected by a tunnel and it had an almost equal wing span to that of the Model 322. The main differences included the use of four Allison in-line engines mounted in tandem and buried in the wing in two nacelles. Two tractor and two pusher propellers provided motive power. The engines were V-1710s, each of 1,150-hp, and were used to power a number of American fighters of the period.

The engine installation of the Model 333 had raised many design problems and had to be highly modified. The final result was the Model 333A and this also had four Allison engines buried in the wings and driving propellers via extension shafts on the wing leading edges. The Allisons lost power rapidly at high altitude and Boeing had to look for a more efficient engine.

The engine chosen for the Model 333B was the new, experimental Wright 'Flat' unit, a type also being developed by Pratt & Whitney. They, too, were buried in the wing and drove the propellers via extension shafts. With the Model 333A wing structure only allowed fuel for a range

Two views of B-24J with the suggestive motto of 'The Dragon and his Tail'. This must have been the most lurid scheme of all. Late production 44-40973, 43rd Bombardment Group.

of 2,500 miles and a completely new wing had to be designed for the Model B. It had to have space for the buried engines and additional fuel to stretch the range to a maximum of 4,500 miles. The design was completed during February 1939.

Within two weeks of their Model 333A/B Boeing produced the Model 334. This was to be powered by the second of the 'Flat' engines, the Pratt & Whitney of 1,800-hp each. They were buried in the wings, which were also of new design, and the empennage had now been changed to a twin fin/rudder assembly. Increased fuel capacity and new wing would have resulted in the stipulated range of 4,500 miles being achieved.

However, despite a maximum speed estimate of 390mph it was

B-24J, 304th Bomb Wing after parachute assisted landing.

decided the 'Flat' engines posed too many production problems. A wooden mock-up had been ordered and on November 10, 1939, General Arnold asked the War Department to issue a Specification for a B-17 replacement with four engines and a range of 2,000 miles plus.

The Super Bomber

Permission was granted for a Fortress replacement on January 29, 1940, with the issue of Data R-40B to all the leading aircraft manufacturers, including Consolidated. The specification called for the 'super' bomber to have a range of 5,333 miles at a cruising speed of 400 mph, and deliver a bomb load of 2,000 lbs. This was to have a profound effect upon the final design stages of the Super Bomber and in the design and production of two aircraft designs, one from Boeing, the second from Consolidated. Probably due to the fact that both companies were in full production with the B-17 and B-24 respectively, any such design would have to be based upon the earlier design in order to speed development.

There were many shades of opinion regarding the need for a bomber larger than the B-17 and B-24. A member of the General Staff declared that the B-17 was much superior to two, or more, smaller twin-engine bombers, but it remained to be established whether there was a real requirement for a larger aircraft than the Fortress. This statement had repercussions as the USAAC was forbidden to purchase additional B-17s over and above the forty already on order. The outbreak of war with the Japanese was to change that decision.

However, when Hitler sent his storm troopers into Czechoslovakia President Roosevelt asked Congress to approve funds for the Air Corps to be equipped with 1,000 bombers. He considered the Corps to be totally inadequate for the role it was intended for, and that the USA had a fifth rate Air Force. Even then Congress considered that America need not be involved in the European War and that additional bombers were not required.

During the same period of time General Marshall, Chief of Staff, declared the new strategy of National Defence would include the whole of the Western Hemisphere. At last the long-range Super Bomber was to be accepted as a necessity.

The place in history of the Consolidated Liberator has been narrated

Two views of B-24M, 451996, with odd fuselage number of BC-922.
Rear view shows tail turret.

above and originally it had not been considered part of the Super Bomber revolution. This was to change when the company accepted the challenge of the Data R-40B specifications which led, ultimately, to the development and final acceptance of the B-32 Dominator as the second super bomber.

Details of the specification reached all of the competing companies, Boeing, Consolidated (Convair), Douglas, Lockheed, North American and Sikorsky and from six designs four were selected as being promising. The USAAC Evaluation Board designated the proposals as follows:- Boeing XB-29, Lockheed XB-30, Douglas XB-31 and Consolidated XB-32, Sikorsky withdrew from the competition as did North American.

For some obscure reason Glenn L. Martin's company, who were building the B-26 Marauder, did not receive the Specification at the same time as the other six companies. Somewhat belatedly they submitted designs which closely resembled the Marauder. The projected XB-33 'Super' Marauder was originally received with enthusiasm by the US Army Air Corps, who immediately gave a contract, No. AC.18645, to cover the design and construction of two prototypes. When the final designs were revealed to the Air Staff the company was awarded a contract for 400 production aircraft straight off the drawing board. Unfortunately the finished aircraft soon proved inadequate and, despite all efforts from the Martin company, the production contract was cancelled.

Of the four remaining contenders the Lockheed XB-30, based upon their civil 'Constellation', was finally rejected as was the design by

B-24M of the 461st Bombardment Group.

Douglas. Their XB-31 was a four-engine version of the A-36 Invader.

The Consolidated Model 33, XB-32, was an obvious development of the B-24 with its refined Davis wing of greater strength and reduced aspect ratio, and the huge, twin fin/rudder assemblies. It featured four 2,300-hp turbo-supercharged, Duplex Cyclone R-3350 engines. It also had a pressure cabin, remote control gun barbettes, all retractable, and an estimated gross weight of 101,000 lbs.

The design was accepted and a contract placed for two, later three, prototype XB-32s on September 9, 1940. This was immediately followed by a contract for 13 YB-32s in June 1941 for use as service test aircraft. The only obvious new design feature was a stepped nose section/cockpit instead of the smooth lines of the prototype.

The prototype had the familiar twin fin/rudder assembly as seen on the B-24 Liberator, while the YBs were to have a large, single fin/rudder which towered over the bomber due to its short fuselage. By the time the prototype was ready for trials the pressure cabin and gun turret installations had to be abandoned as problems had become insurmountable. Prototype serial 41-141 was rolled out of the San Diego factory approximately six months behind schedule.

Two Wright R-3350 engines were installed inboard and two R-3350-1, outboard on the wings all driving three bladed Hamilton Standard Hydromatic propellers. Further delays led to the prototype's first flight being put off until September 7, 1942, but trouble loomed again as the rudders were not working correctly and the flight terminated after only twenty minutes. An emergency landing was made at NAS North Island.

In February 1943 the YB-32 contract was suddenly cancelled but confidence in the design returned when an order for 300 B-32s, with the new tall tail fin assembly, was placed and the name Terminator adopted.

Modified B-24H with remote control side gun turrets.

On May 10 the first prototype crashed killing the pilot. The second machine, 41-142, flew on July 2, 1942.

USAAC now had, for two reasons, a change of heart. The B-29 prototypes had flown and although not 100 percent perfect had performed better than the XB-32 and contracts for the latter were cancelled. It was reported that the Air Force had stated the XB-32 was obsolete to requirements but recommended a large number of modifications. This included an armament of eight x 0.50in machine guns in dorsal and ventral turrets and one 20mm cannon in each outboard engine nacelle firing toward the rear, all controlled by aiming stations in the fuselage and tail. A further two 0.50in guns were installed in the wing leading edge outboard of the engines.

For production aircraft the armament was changed to ten x 0.50in machine guns paired in power operated turrets in nose, dorsal, ventral and tail positions. The pressurised system was abandoned and bomb load increased from 4,000 to 12,000 lbs. Four bladed propellers replaced the originals.

B-24 with ventral radar pod.

Stability problems with the second prototype XB-32 during trials resulted in a redesign of the tailplane and fins, and when it flew again after making 25 flights, the double fin/rudders had been replaced by a direct copy of the single fin/rudder of its rival, the B-29.

This was inadequate for the XB-32 which was bulkier than the XB-29 with its refined fuselage and the decision was taken to redesign a second time resulting in the single fin/rudder being over 19 feet tall and similar to that of the company's PB4Y Privateer. The new arrangement was first flown on the third prototype 41-108836 on November 3, 1943.

Despite the fact that the new single fin was proven to be successful the first production B-32 Terminator, 42-108471, flew with the XB-29 copy.

With all these revisions of design the aircraft was re-designated as the Model 34, and production orders were re-instated when a third contract was placed for 1,500 aircraft. It appeared that the B-32 was to be the second Super Bomber alongside the B-29.

However, a major problem for this contract was for 500 to be produced at the San Diego plant along with fuselage sections for a Fort Worth factory. It appeared to be a complicated arrangement. The power-plant auxiliaries were built at Downey, while the Stinson Division of Consolidated built the fin/rudder assemblies.

Engines for the contract were shipped directly from the Chicago factory of General Motors. In August 1944 the name Terminator was

PB4Y-2 shows the armament positions.

changed to Dominator as certain members of Congress objected to a name suggesting such aggression. One year later, in August 1945, the US State department objected to the name of Dominator and it was dropped in favour of calling the new bomber by its designation, B-32.

First deliveries were made on September 10, 1944, with the second, Fort Worth built 42-10842, but during its delivery flight it crashed and was written off. By the following December only five B-32s had been delivered, its record compared unfavourably with that of the B-29 which was now in full service and bombing Japan.

Service trials of production aircraft (the YB-32s) had been cancelled and were made at various USAAF technical bases such as Wright Field and Elgin to test production aircraft. The 40 aircraft 42-10485 to 10824 were delivered as TB-32s without armament and used for the B-29 training programme.

The B-32, like a number of its contemporaries were too late. The B-29 meanwhile had progressed in a series of steady design stages from the XB-15, through the XB-17 and a great number of project drawings, and several proposals had been examined. Although in the early stages of its trials programme, the B-29 had its own problems, the Boeing team's experience with production of a large number of bombers enabled them to cure virtually every fault, including persistent engine fires.

On the B-32 the aircraft did possess several excellent features, but its

PB4Y-2 of French Navy Escadrille, 1953

faults were too numerous for them to be overcome before the bomber was rushed into service. The most noticeable were high noise levels in the cockpit, poor instrument layout, bad bombardier position and, more seriously, gross overweight. As with the B-29 engine fires with the Wright engines would not be eradicated in time.

Finally the complete batch of B-32 production aircraft was grounded in May 1945 due to undercarriage failures.

Production models differed from the prototypes in having more powerful engines, reversible thrust inner propellers, front ball turret, twin dorsal powered turrets, plus one ventral, retractable unit. The rear defence was also increased by a single 'stinger'. However, the aircraft lacked the pressure facility of the B-29 and as a result it was used only briefly for operations against the Japanese and was eventually down-graded for use as a crew trainer for the B-29. A rather sad end for an inspired design.

However, such was the urgency to continue the high rate of attack on Japanese held islands in the Pacific and on the mainland that a number of

PBY-1. Yellow overall. Converted by US Navy modification unit.

B-32s were despatched to the Philippines for combat trials. Six additional machines arrived on May 29, 1945, and all were taken on charge by the 396th Bomb Squadron at Floridablanca.

In August 1945 the Squadron moved to Okinawa as soon as the island had been occupied by MacArthur's ground forces. From there they flew photographic reconnaissance missions with the last taking place on August 28, 1945. Two aircraft were lost and after VJ-Day, within the same month, the squadron was re-routed back to America.

All production contracts were cancelled in September 1945 and, in addition to the forty that had been delivered from Forth Worth, 74 had been completed as 42-108471 to 108484 and 108515 to 108584. San Diego produced just one, 44-904486. A number were put into long term storage at Kingman, Arizona, but the majority were scrapped.

One private company, Reynolds, proposed a plan to fly the B-32 around the world, over both polar regions, but this plan was abandoned. Another example was intended for display at the Air Force Museum but that idea was scrapped in August 1949.

So ended what was a great disappointment to both the USAAF and Consolidated. The Liberator was a great aeroplane, but its successor was designed and rushed into service long before it was ready.

After the war a number of Liberators were converted for civil use.

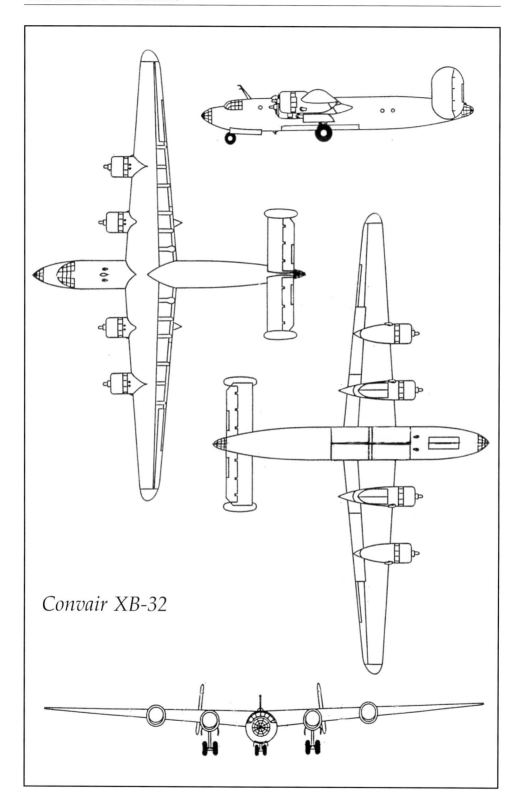

Convair XB-32

CHAPTER ELEVEN

Camouflage and Markings

Camouflage

The paint finish requirement for USAAC aircraft, especially for fighters and bombers serving in the European Theatre of Operations (ETO), was quoted as 'Basic Camouflage Scheme' and read as follows.

> The camouflage finish for Army Air Force aircraft is to be Dark Olive Drab, Shade No.41, for surfaces viewed from above and extending down the sides of the fuselage. Medium Green, Shade No.42, in irregular patches along the leading and trailing edges of the upper surface of the wing and the horizontal outline of the tail assembly. This should also be carried along all edges of both sides of the vertical outline of the tail assembly, extending inwards from the edges of various distances up to 20 percent of the total width of the wing or tail assembly. Rubber parts are not to be painted except when utilising de-ice paint in White camouflage. Neutral Oyster Shade Grey, Shade No.43, will be used for surfaces viewed from below. Masking will not be employed to separate ANY COLOURS. Junction lines will be blended by over-spraying.

That was the declared basic camouflage scheme. All upper surfaces in dark Olive Drab with irregular splotches of Medium Green along all wing edges, back and front undersides in Neutral Grey.

Medium Green, Shade 42, was used on upper wing and fuselages for aircraft operating over terrain predominantly green. Sand, Shade 40, was used for upper surfaces of aircraft operating over desert terrain. A Pink overall was also used later in the war for aircraft in this theatre.

Black, Shade 44, was for under surfaces of aircraft to be used for night flying. The use of any camouflage materials in colour was covered in Bulletin No.41. This specified lacquer, No. 14105, dope, No.14106, and enamel, No. 14109, could be used for aircraft in Alaskan or other theatres

B-24J-1 in all Glossy Black scheme for night bombing. Note the modified nose section.

having similar terrain conditions. The final instructions allowed aircraft of the commanding officers of the Desert Liberators to be painted Pink overall.

Under surfaces could be Insignia White, Shade 46, on all under surfaces and leading edges, and Olive Drab, Shade 41, on all upper surfaces for aircraft used for research purposes. Special de-icing paint in Oyster White was available for this and other camouflage outlines.

B-24M, 461st Bombardment Group, with Red tail markings. Note feathered propeller.

B-24 late production mode, serial 442691

However, it is an established fact that the scheme for all anti-submarine aircraft, including the Liberator, was a Dull Dark Grey on all upper surfaces with Dull Grey Light on under surfaces, extending up the whole fuselage to the Dull dark Grey uppers. Fins in Dull Grey Dark.

White non-specular was to be applied to the fuselage sides under the wing root extending down to the bottom fuselage of White Glossy camouflage. Coastal Command, RAF, painted their Liberators Dull Grey on all upper surfaces and White on under surfaces.

As an emergency rejuvenator for old fabric, ailerons, elevators, rudders the following formula was recommended.

To one gallon of 2 to 1 mix of clear dope, Specification AN-TT-T-258, and blush retarding thinner, Specification AN-TT-T-258, add one fluid ounce of tri-grey phosphate and castor oil. Apply one coat by brush to clean surface followed by one spray coat. After several hours of drying spray one coat of aluminised dope.

For removal of all types of paint material from metal surfaces it recommended the following.

Use paint or varnish remover, Specification No.14119. For removal of dope from fabric surfaces use nitrate dope and lacquer thinner. Specification AN-TT-T-256.

Markings

Each part and assembly will be permanently and legibly marked in the same manner as the drawings numbers. Various detail and codes, as required by Specification No.98-24105Q, will be maintained. Use one coat of varnish Specification TT-V-121. Painting of engine cowlings in colours authorised by the Commanding Officer. Standard national insignia designated by the Commanding General will be used.

APPENDIX A

B-24s built at the San Diego, California, plant

XB-24   One built under Contract 12436 dated 30 March 1939. Delivered 16 August 1940.

YB-24   Contract 12464 of 26 April 1939, serials 39-681 to 687 One only delivered of 5 April 1941. Later redesignated as RB-24. Six to RAF.

LB-30A   Contract 12464 of 26 April 1939 for six aircraft. Ordered by France, serials 40-696 to 701. Diverted to RAF under Contract BR-5068 (British) on 16 December 1940 with British serials AM258 to 262.

LB-30B   Contract BR-F-677 for 20 aircraft on 4 June 1939. Originally ordered by France.

B-24A   Contract 13281 for nine aircraft on 10 August 1939. Order revised for 38 as B-24A. Some as B-24C/D. Serials 40—2369 to 2377.

LB-30.   Contract BR-F-677 of 10 August 1939 for 104 aircraft. To RAF as Liberator Mk.II. USAAF had 75.

B-24C   Contract 13281 for nine aircraft on 12 September 1939. Serials 40-2378 to 2386.

B-24D   Contract 12464 for six aircraft on 26 April 1939. Serials 40-696 60 701.

B-24D   Contract 13281 for six aircraft on 12 September 1939. Serials 40-2349 to 2355.

B-24D   Contract 13281 for 303 aircraft on 18 September 1940. Eight as CF. 41-11678 as XB-24F. 41-11822 as XB-41.

B-24D   Contract DA-4 for 629 aircraft on 12 May 1941. Serials 41-23640 to 24269. 43 as Privateer PB4Y-1 for US Navy.

B-24-D.   Contract 24620. First mass production model for 1200 examples on 19 February 1942. Serials 42-40058 to 41257. 42-40254 as AB-24K. 44-40344 as XB-24P. One as PB4Y-1.

B-24J.   Contract 30461 for 199 on 29 June 1942. Serials 42-72765 to 72963. Twenty one as PB4Y-1.

B-24J. Contract 30461 for 551 aircraft on 21 November 1942. Serials 42-72964 to 75314. Fifty four as PB4Y-1. One with Fortress nose section. 42-73215 with General Electric fitted TG-180 turbuprop engines.

B-24J. Contract 35312 for 900 aircraft on 29 June 1942, serials 42-99936 to 100435 and 42-109789 to 110118. 78 as PB4Y-1.

B-24J. Largest B-24 Contract, 40033 for 1341 examples. Serials 44-40049 to 41389. 258 as PB4Y-1.

B-24L. Contract 40033 for 417 aircraft on 21 Devcember 1943, serials 44-41390 to 41806. Total of 86 with hand held guns. 186 as PB4Y-1.

B-24M. Contract 40033 for 916 aircraft on 21 December 1943. Serials 44-41807 to 42711 as PB4Y-1. Grand total built at San Diego 6726.

B-24s built at the Fort Worth, Texas, plant

B-24D. Contract 18723 of 20 May 1941, 8 aircraft. Contract for 8 aircraft. Contract 26992 for 295 aircraft, serials 41-63752 to 64046. Four as PB4Y-1.

B-24E. Contract 18723 of 26 September 1941 for 107 aircraft, serials 41-29009 to 29115. Contract 26992 for 37 aircraft, serials 42-64395 to 64431.

B-24H. Contract 26992 of 29 May 1942 for 70 aircraft, serials 42-64432 to 64502. Contract 18723 of 26 September 1941 for 493 aircraft, serials 41-29116 to 29608.

B-24J. Contract 26992 for 348 aircraft, serials 42-64047 to 64394. 42-64175 as F-7A. Contract 26992 of 21 November 1942 for 200 aircraft, serials 42-99736 to 99935. Contract 40715 of 18 February 1944 for 500 aircraft, serials 44-10253 to 10752. Contract 18723 for 57 aircraft, serials 44-10253 to 10303. Contract 40023 of 21 December 1943 for 453 aircraft, serials 44-44049 to 44501. RAF/RCAF.

B-24s built at the Tulsa, Oklahoma, plant

B-24D. + Contract 18722 of 20 May 1941 for 10 aircraft, serials 41-11754 to 11763 and 11864.

B-24E.   Contract 18722 of 20 May 1941 for 167 aircraft, serials 41-28409 to 228573 and 41-29007 to 29008.

B-24H.   Contract 18722 of 20 May 1941 for 433 aircraft, serials 28574 to 29006. Contract 18722 of 11 April 1942 for 149 aircraft, serials 42-51077 to 51225.

B-24J.   Contract 18722 of 11 April 1942 for 205 aircraft, serials 42-51266 to 51471.

Subsequent orders for 646 aircraft were cancelled.

B-24s built at Willow Run

Willow Run was the largest aircraft factory built in America specifically for Liberator production.

B-24E.   Contract 21216 for 490 aircraft, serials 42-6976 to 7474. 42-7221 as XC-109.

B-24H.   Contract 21216 for 305 aircraft on 26 September 1941, serials 42-7465 to 7769. Contract 21216 for 700 aircraft on 11 April 1942, serials 42-52077 to 52776. Contract 21216 for 775 aircraft on 10 August 1942, serials 42-94727 to 95503.

B-24J.   Contract for 125 aircraft on 10 August 1942 for 125 aircraft, serials 42-95509 to 95628. Contract 21216 for 1214 aircraft on 22 June 1944, serials 42-50509 to 51076 and 42- 51431 to 52076.

B-24L.   Contract 21216 for 1250 aircraft on 19 January 1944, serials 44-9002 to 50251

B-24M.   Contract 21216 for 1,677 aircraft on 19 January 1944, serials 44-50252 to 51929.

XB-24N.   Contract 21216 for one aircraft on 28 January 1944. Serial 44-48753.

YB-24N.   Contract 21216 for seven aircraft on 19 January 1944, serials 44-52053 to 52059.

B-24G.   Contract 14663 for 430 aircraft on 1 May 1942, serials 42-78045 to 78454. First 25 as B-24D, rest B-24J.

B-24J.   Contract 24663 for 536 aircraft on 10 december 1942, serials 42-78475 to 78794 and 44-28061 to 28276.

Total of 18,482 aircraft built. Cost of building each Liberator was $215,516 each, as compared with the Fortress at $187,742.

APPENDIX B

Liberator variants

XB-24 Model 32.

YB-24 Seven service trial models.

LB-30 Transport version of the Liberator Mk.II.

LB-30A For RAF as transport, similar to the YB-24.

Liberator Mk.I

Liberator Mk.II

Liberator C.Mk.IX (LB-30)

B-24A First USAAC model.

XB-24B First prototype with elliptical engine cowlings.

B-24C Production B-24B with gun turrets.

Liberator Mk.III RAF version of B-24D.

Liberator Mk.IIA Lend-Lease model.

Liberator Mk.V Ford built B-24E.

B-24B Firstmass production model.

Liberator C.Mk.VII (C-97) Express US Navy RV-2.

XF-7 Conversion of 24D to PR variant

XB-24F Test aircraft for de-icing trials.

B-24E Test aircraft for de-icing trials.

B-24G Longer fuselage and nose gun turret.

B-24H Mass production model developed from 24G. RAF Liberator Mk.IV.

XB-24K B-24D with nose gun turret.

Liberator Mk.IV

Liberator GR.Mk.IV Additional fuel, radar. Leight Lights, ASV.

C-109 Fuel tanker.

B-24J Mass production model. Liberator Mk.VI.

GR.Mk.V Coastal Command

EZB-24 Aero Icing Research Laboratory.

Liberator Mk.VI

C.Mk.VI Transport

GR.Mk.VI

Liberastor C.Mk.VII RV-2 US Navy.

Liberator Mk.VIII

Liberator C.Mk.IX

PB4Y-1 US Navy variant.

AT-22 Advanced trainer.

C-87 Liberator Express.

C-87A VIP sleeper.

RY-1 For US Navy.

F.7 PR conversion.

F-7A Rebuild of B-24J.

F.7B Rebuild of B-24J.

B-24K First single fin prototype.

B-24L Manual control tail guns.

RV-24L B-29 gunnery trials.

B-24M Lightweight tail gun turret.

YB-24N Service test aircraft for B-24N.

PB4Y-2 For US Navy.

C-87 RY-3.

SB-24 Special radar sight.

XC-109 Fuel tanker.

XP-24Q Removal of tail guns.

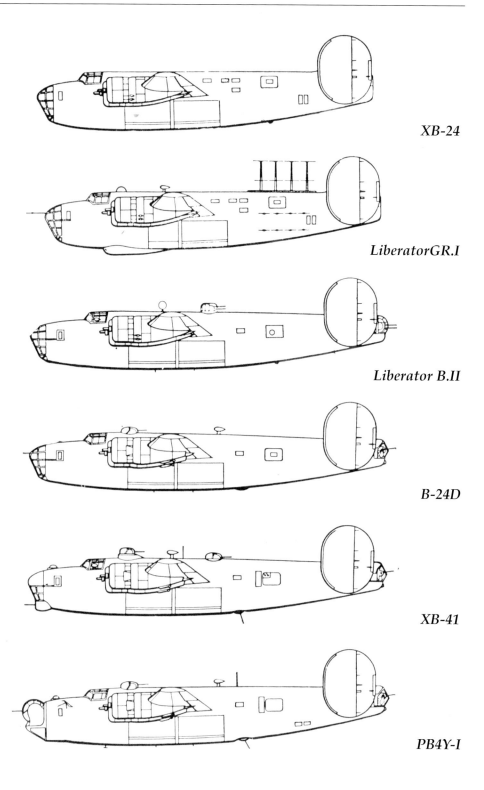

XB-24

LiberatorGR.I

Liberator B.II

B-24D

XB-41

PB4Y-I

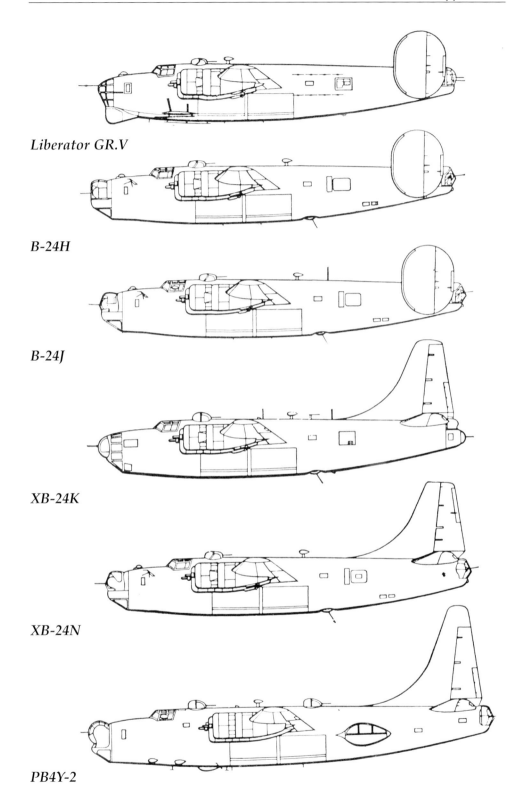

Liberator GR.V

B-24H

B-24J

XB-24K

XB-24N

PB4Y-2

APPENDIX C

USAAC/USAAF Organisation

During World War Two the American Air Corps was organised in the following manner.

First Air Force.
Constituted October 1940.

Second Air Force.
Constituted October 1940.

Third Air Force.
Constituted as Southwest Air District, October 1940, but became the Third in 1941.

Fourth Air Force.
Constituted October 1940 as Southwest Air District and became the Fourth in 1941.

Fifth Air Force.
Formed in the Philippines in August 1941.

Sixth Air Force.
Constituted as the Panama Canal Air Force and became the Sixth in February 1942.

Seventh Air Force.
Started life as the Hawaiian Air Force to become the seventh.

Eighth Air Force.
Probably the most well known of all the American Air Forces and was originally called VIII Bomber Command. Operated initially for the bombing of Europe.

Ninth Air Force.
Another well known force activated September 1941 and formed part of the Tactical Air Force, Europe, for the Invasion of Europe.

Tenth Air Force.
Formed in February 1942 and fought in India and the Far East.

Eleventh Air Force.
Formed as Alaska Air Force and became the Alaskan Air Command.

Twelfth Air Force.
Activated in August 1942 and after arriving in England was transferred to North Africa.

Fourteenth Air Force.
Fought in China against the Japanese.

Fifteenth Air Force.
Activated October 1943 and went to the Middle East (MTO).

Twentieth Air Force.
The Air Force than changed for ever the nature of Strategic Bombing when it attacked Hiroshima and Nagasaki with the first atomic bombs.

APPENDIX D

USAAC and Associated Groups with their squadrons equipped with the B-24.

Air Force	Bomb Groups	Bomb Squadrons
5th Air Force	22nd	2nd, 19th, 33rd, 408th
	43rd	63rd, 64th, 65th, 403rd
	90th	319th, 320th, 321st, 400th
	380th	528th, 529th, 530th, 532nd.
7th Air Force	11th	26th, 42nd, 98th, 431st.
	30th	27th, 39th, 393rd, 819th.
	494th	864th, 865th, 866th, 867th.
8th Air Force		
2nd Bomber Wing	389th	564th, 565th, 566th, 567th.
	455th	700th, 701st, 702nd, 703rd.
	453rd	732nd, 733rd, 734th, 735th.
14th Bomber Wing	44th	66th, 67th, 68th, 508th.
	392nd	576th, 577th, 578th, 579th.
	492nd	856th, 857th, 858th, 859th.
20th Bomb Wing	93rd	328th, 329th, 330th, 40th.
	446th	704th, 705th, 706th, 707th.

20th Bomb Wing Cont.	448th	712th, 713th, 714th, 715th.
92nd Bomb Wing	486th	832nd, 833rd, 834th, 835th.
	487th	836th, 837th, 838th, 839th.
93rd Bomb Wing	34th	4th, 7th, 18th, 391st.
	490th	848th, 849th, 850th, 851sr.
	493rd	860th, 861st, 862nd, 863rd.
95th Bomb Wing	489th	844th, 845th, 846th. 847th
	491st	852nd, 853rd, 854th, 856th.
9th Air Force	9th	343rd, 344th, 345th, 346th.
	376th	512th, 513th, 514th, 515th.
10th Air Force	7th	26th, 42nd, 98th, 431st.
11th Air Force	28th Com. Group	77th, 404th.
12th Air Force	As for 9th Air Force	
13th Air Force	5th	23rd, 31st, 72nd, 394th.
	307th	370th, 371st, 373rd, 424th.
14th Air Force	308th	373rd, 374th, 375th, 425th.
15th Air Force		
47th Bomb Wing	98th	343rd, 344th, 345th, 415th.
	376th	512th, 513rd, 514th, 515th.
	449th	716th, 717th, 718th, 719th.
	450th	720th, 721st, 722nd, 723rd.
49th Bomb Wing	451st	724th, 725th, 726th, 727th.

49th Bomb Wing Cont.	461st	764th, 765th, 766th, 747th.
	484th	824th, 825th, 826th, 827th
55th Bomb Wing	460th	760th, 761st, 762nd, 763rd.
	464th	776th, 777th, 778th, 779th.
	465th	781st, 782nd, 783rd, 784th.
	485th	828th, 829th, 830th, 831st.
304th Bomb Wing	454th	736th, 737th, 738th, 739th.
	455th	740th, 741st, 742nd, 743rd.
	456th	744th, 745th, 746th, 747th.
	459th	756th, 757th, 758th, 759th.

APPENDIX E

USAAF B-24 Squadrons

When the American Force constituted the many fighter and bomber squadrons they were normally activated as and when they were required for service. In the immediate and early days of the war the squadrons were issued as single units as America was not involved in the war and the long range B-17 Fortress was regarded as a weapon of defence against any seaborne attempt at invasion of the American homeland. A force in the early 1940s would have little, or no, air arm other than those carried aboard the aircraft carrier. The only nation that had that force was Japan and the American government headed by Franklin Roosevelt was aware that it was a nation that could be tempted to procure a foothold into the Western Pacific. With this possibility in mind BuAer (Bureau of Aeronautics) launched a competition for a heavy bomber with a longer range than the Fortress.

This aircraft was the B-24 Liberator and during the subsequent war that followed from 1939 to 1945, the Liberator was regarded as the best weapon with which to counter the aggression in the Pacific. At no time did the Americans envisage that both the B-17 and B-24 would also be the long range bombers that would help eventually defeat the Hitlerite Germany.

ETO signified that the squadron operated in the European Theatre Operations which included France, Germany and her satellites. MTO signified the Mediterranean Theatre of Operations and this included the Middle East, Western Desert, East Africa and Italy. PTO was the Pacific Theatre of Operations. A number of squadrons were to be formed later in the war without any specific aircraft and as such never entered service but were regarded as being available should there be a need for additional squadrons. As the war progressed whole batches of squadrons were constituted and activated and then issued to Groups and Wings.

The Liberator was a fine aeroplane, fast, heavily armed with a high altitude performance and its range was such that the whole of Europe was within its area of operations. However, it had two, major faults. On many B-24s the wing would, when damaged, fold back alongside the fuselage. The second fault was the large, twin fin/rudder assemblies. If one was heavily damaged or destroyed the aeroplane was uncontrollable. The Fortress had a large, generous fin/rudder area which could absorb a lot of punishment. Indeed, there are instances of the B-17 making the journey from Germany back to base with a large area of the fin shot away.

There follows a list of B-24 Liberator squadrons that served with the USAAF and other air forces, in particular, the Royal Air Force in Bomber and Coastal Command. In the latter it helped defeat the German U-boat campaign.

1st Anti-submarine.
Activated January 1942. Carried out A-S operations in ETO and MTO.

2nd Bombardment.
Activated February 1940. Anti-submarine duties in South-West and Western Pacific.

3rd Bombardment.
Activated February 1940. Anti-submarine patrols. Replacement training.

3rd Sea-Search/Attack.
Activated December 1942. Training squadron for electronic equipment.

4th Anti-submarine.
Activated January 1941. A-S operations in American Theatre. ETO. A-S in EAME.

4th Search Attack.
Activated July 1942. Training squadron

5th Bombardment.
Training Unit. A-S patrols. PTO.

6th Anti-submarine.
Activated January 1941 A-S patrols American Theatre. ETO.

6th Bombardment.
Activated February 1940.

7th Bombardment.
Activate January 1941. A-S patrols. ETO.

9th Bombardment.
PTO, MTO.

11th Bombardment.
A-S patrols American Theatre with LB-30. PTO. CBI India.

14th Anti-submarine.
Activated October 1942. A-S patrols

18th Bombardment.
Activated 15 January 1941. A-S patrols. ETO

19th Anti-submarine.
Activated July 1942. PTO.

21st Bombardment.
A-S patrols. PTO.

25th, 26th, 27th Bombardment.
PTO.

29th Bombardment.
Activated April 1941 A-S patrols. Replacement training.

31st Bombardment.
Activated April 11931. PTO.

33rd Bombardment.
Activated February 1940. A-S patrols. PTO.

36th Bombardment.
Activated February 1940. PTO. ETO (Carpetbagger operations).

38th Bombardment.
Activated January 1941. A-S patrols. Replacement training.

42nd Bombardment.
Activated February 1940. PTO.

43rd Bombardment.
Activated February 1940. A-S patrols. PTO.

44th Bombardment.
Activated April 1941. A-S patrols. CBI, PTO.

45th Bombardment.
Activated June 1942. MTO, ETO.

52nd Bombardment.
Activated February 1940. American Theatre.

60th Bombardment.
Activated January 1941. MTO.

61st Bombardment.
Activated January 1941. PTO.

62nd, 63rd, 64th, 65th Bombardment.
Activated January 1941. PTO.

66th, 67th, 68th Bombardment.
Activated January 1941. ETO, MTO.

69th Bombardment.
Activated January 1941. PTO.

72nd Bombardment.
Activated May 1923. PTO.

74th Bombardment.
Activated October 1933. A-S patrols. Replacement training.

75th Bombardment.
Activated January 1941. A-S patrols. PTO.

97th Bombardment.
Activated January 1941. A-S patrols MTO.

98th Bombardment.
Activated December 1941. PTO.

There was a large gap between the 100 and 300th squadrons

319th, 320th Bombardment.
Activated April 1942. PTO.

322nd Bombardment.
Activated April 1942. ETO.

328th Bombardment.
Activated May 1942. ETO.

330th Bombardment.
Activated March 1943. A-S patrols. ETO.

343rd, 344th, 345th Bombardment.
Activated February 1942. ETO, MTO.

355th Bombardment.
Activated June 1942. Training. PTO.

356th, 357th Bombardment.
Activated June 1942. PTO.

370th Bombardment.
Activated April 1942. PTO. Training.

APPENDIX F

Royal Air Force B-24 Squadrons

The Royal Air Force first received the B-24 Liberator when six were diverted to transport duties between Prestwick, Newfoundland and Montreal to form the trans-Atlantic return Ferry Service operated by BOAC. This service flew RAF ferry pilots to Canada to collect and fly back to Britain numbers of American aircraft for the RAF.

The Liberators were designated as the LB-30A (Liberator Mk.I) and as a result of consultations with the British Commission in America improved the operational efficiency of the B-24 by adding defensive guns, armour plate and non-inflammable, self-seal fuel tanks.

Liberator Mk.Is entered service with RAF Coastal Command with No. 120 Squadron in June 1941, which was based at Nutts Corner, near Belfast, Northern Island to become the first VLR (Very Long Range) aircraft. This was followed by the Mk.II which also went into service with No.120 Squadron. The type also equipped Nos. 59 and 86 Squadrons.

In the Middle East the Mk.II was flown by Nos. 259 and 160 Squadrons which became operational in June 1942. The B-24D was also the RAF's Liberator Mk.III used by Coastal Command as a VLR, and the first Lend-Lease Liberator supplied to the RAF was the Mark IIIA. There followed the B-24H and J which, in Coastal Command service became known as the Gr.Mk.VI. The GR Mk.V was the B-24G, a number of which were equipped with Leigh Lights.

The final variant of the Liberator for Coastal Command was the GR.Mk.VIII. It was a successful weapon insofar as Coastal Command was concerned that sank seven U-boars in the Atlantic. The Liberator Mk.VI flew with No.178 Squadron in the Middle East. Also, Liberators Mk.VI ands Mk.VIII flew with No.184 Wing of the North Borneo Air Task Force. The Mks. GRV and VI were based in Ceylon with No. 222 Group RAF for anti-submarine duties over the Indian Ocean.

The various transport Liberators were known as the C.Mk.VII and served with Nos.46 Group Transport Command. The final transport was the C.Mk.IX which entered service with No.45 Group Command in Canada.

From March 1941 Coastal Command flew Liberators to well after the war had ended until eventually replacing them with the Shackleton when they were withdrawn from service in June 1946. A detailed list of RAF Liberator squadrons follows, emphasising that there were squadrons that flew the bomber as reconnaissance types.

R.A.F. Liberator Squadrons

No. 37
An old squadron originally formed in 1916 and became a Reserve Squadron. Reformed in 1935 with the Heyford and eventually with the Liberator B.Mk.VI in October 1944. It took part in the MTO (Middle East Theatre).

No. 40
Formed in February 1916 it operated during the First World War as a fighter squadron before being reformed as a bomber unit based at Upper Heyford. During the Second World War it flew such types as the Fairey Gordon, Hart bomber, Battle and Blenheim and Wellington medium before receiving its Liberator Mk.VIs in March 1945, mainly in the Mediterranean until January 1946. The squadron's last mission with the Liberator was a raid in April 1945 on the marshalling yards at Frielassing, Germany. Code letter BL.

No. 53
Coastal Command.

No. 70
Formed part of the Royal Flying Corps in France in April 1916 and was engaged in bombing and reconnaissance duties. In February 1921 No.58 Squadron was renumbered as No.70 with H.P. 0/400 and Vimy bombers in Egypt until re-equipping with the Wellington in September 1940. It moved to Italy in 1943 and flew the Liberator B.Mk.VI bomber in January 1945. The last attack by Liberators of this unit was on the night of 25/26 April 1945. Code letters DU.

No. 86
Coastal Command.

No. 99
(Madras Presidency). Established during August 1917 and was posted

overseas with the D.H.9 bomber as part of the Independent Force to be engaged in long distance attacks on German cities. After the war it was sent to India and in 1924 was reformed and flew the Vimy and Heyford heavy bombers until the Second World War, when it took delivery of the Wellington. It moved overseas again to India to take part in operations against the Japanese in Burma. After exchanging the Wellington for the Liberator B.Mk.VI it made a number of long distance raid against the Siam-Burma railway. It final base was in the Pacific was on the Cocos Islands. Code letters VF and LN.

No. 103
Flew the Halifax and Lancaster and had one or two Liberators on strength.

No. 104
This R.F.C. squadron was formed in September 1917 and were equipped with the D.H.9 bomber in the Independent Force which attacked Germany. It was reformed in January 1936 as No.104 Squadron and served with No.6 Group as a training squadron. In 1941 it was activated as a bomber squadron with the Wellington as part of No.4 Group. It served in the Middle East in Italy, Sicily, Crete and much of North Africa with the Wellington. It was not equipped with the Liberator Mk.VII (FE) until February 1945, using it to attack marshalling yards in Germany and drop supplies for Allied forces in Northern Italy. Code letter PO and EP.

No. 108
Yet another bomber squadron formed in November 1917 with the D.H.9 for bombing targets in Belgium. It was reformed in January 1937 at Upper Heyford and was also to be transferred to No.6 Group as a training squadron. In August 1941 it was stationed in Egypt with the Wellington which it exchanged for the Liberator Mk.II in December 1941. Its final mission in the Middle East was in November 1942. Code letters MF for a period.

No. 120
Coastal Command.

No. 148
Became part of the R.F.C. in February 1918 and flew the Vickers F.E.2b bomber. It was reformed at Scampton in June 1937 as a long range bomber unit with light bombers such as the Hart. It also flew the Heyford bomber and the Wellington medium, and when moving to Egypt supported the 8th Army in the desert campaign against the Afrika Korps It was equipped with the Liberator in June 1945 and operated as a Special Duties squadron, dropping supplies to partisans in the Balkans. After the war it became established as a heavy bomber unit based in Italy before disbanding in November 1945. Code letters BS.

Liberator B.Mk.VI of No. 355 Squadron, Salbani, India.

No. 159

One of a small number of Bomber Command squadrons that was supplied with the Liberator B.Mk.II when it was formed in January 1942. It was transferred to the Middle east but diverted to India during the journey between February/May 1942. It played its part in the many desert campaigns in North Africa, Sicily, Southern Greece and the

B.Mk.VIII Liberator of No. 215 Squadron, India.

Mediterranean. The following November it was transferred to Burma as part of a year of movement. From April 1945 it became part of the Pathfinder Force and mined Penang Harbour in October 1944. The normal bomb load for long range operations was 3,000 lbs, but this was to be raised by careful modification such as the removal of some equipment and use of fuel in the cruise mode. Its final duties were as an aerial survey aircraft with the last operation carried out in August 1945 when it bombed targets in Siam/Burma.

No. 160

Formed in January 1942 with the Liberator Mk.II and became attached to No.120 (General Reconnaissance) Squadron. Its first operation was providing air cover for the Malta convoys and it remained in the Middle East attacking German forces in the desert. It followed these with similar operations in Italy. Later stationed in Ceylon with No.22 Group for anti-submarine patrol, minelaying and Special Operations.

No. 178

Formed in the Middle East at Shandur in the Suez Canal Zone, Egypt, on 15 January 1943 as a heavy bomber squadron and took part in all the major desert war operations in North Africa. It also attacked targets in the Balkans, including the Ploesti oil fields when attached to the American 15th Air Force. Final operations were ferrying supplies to the 8th Army when it advanced in Austria.

No. 200 and 206
Coastal Command.

No. 215

Originally formed in March 1918 as part of the Royal Naval Air Service and also became part of the Independent Force, 83rd Wing, with Handley Page 0/100 bombers. It was first equipped with the Liberator Mk.VI and Mk.VIII in August 1942 and flew missions against the Japanese. Final attack on Japanese held bridge on 8 April 1945. Code letters BH and LG.

No. 223 (100 Group)

Was formed in 1917 and disbanded after the war in 1919. Was reformed in Kenya and fought the Second World War in Egypt. It became a support unit in No.100 Group to fly modified B-17s and B-24s for Special duties equipped with electronic gear. Dropped Window in a final raid against Keil.

No. 232 and 246
Served as Transport Squadrons.

No. 301 Polish.
Flew the Wellington bomber before becoming part of Coastal Command.

No. 355
Was formed in August 1943 at Salbani, India. Its first operational mission was on November 19/20, 1943, when three Liberators bombed the railway station at Mandalay. Its last mission was on August 7, 1945, when four Liberators bombed shipping off the east coast of Kra Isthmus and went on to bomb the Siam-Burma railway in the Bangkok area. The squadron was disbanded at the end of May 1946.

No. 358
This squadron equipped with the Liberator B.Mk.VI, formed on 8 November 1944 and disbanded just one year later. It operated in India and flew Special duty missions against Japanese-held Indo-China. Its final operation was bombing Mandalay in January 1945, after which it was stood down.

No. 547
Coastal Command.

No. 614
Formed in Cardiff in June 1937 as an Auxiliary Air Force Army Co-op squadron, one of the first. In early 1945 the squadron switched from the Halifax to the Liberator and was used as a Tactical Bomber unit in support of Allied ground forces in Europe. When the war ended it transported servicemen back to the U.K for demobilising. It was part of the Pathfinder Force for raids over Germany and final operations in the same area.

The Liberator served in many Royal Air Force Bomber Command Groups:- Nos.1, 2, 3, 4, 5, 6 (RCAF), and 8 Pathfinder Force.